UNPOISONING THE WELL

D. C. Zook

SHANTIWALA
BOOKS

Berkeley, CA

Aside from brief quotations for media coverage and reviews, no part of this book may be reproduced or distributed in any form without the author's permission.

Text copyright © 2018 by D. C. Zook
All rights reserved.
Published by Shantiwala Books (Berkeley, CA)
Cover design by James, GoOnWrite.com
ISBN-13 (print): 9781947609112
ISBN-13 (E-book): 9781947609037
ISBN-10: 1947609114

Ourselves Among Others:
The Extravagant Failure of Diversity in America
and An Epic Plan to Make It Work

Understanding the Misunderstanding (vol. 1)

Liberating the Enclave (Vol. 2)

Writing the Past Imperfect (vol. 3)

Unpoisoning the Well (vol. 4)

To the spirit and memory of Pramoedya Ananta Toer, who never lost hope in justice and never gave up on humanity

TABLE OF CONTENTS

Preface to Part 4	Unpoisoning the Well	ix
Chapter 1	The Work of Diversity	1
Chapter 2	Courting Diversity	72
Chapter 3	Confronting Diversity	97
Chapter 4	Testing Diversity	120
Chapter 5	Rewarding Diversity	151
Epilog	Unpoisoning the Well	171
Index		185
About the Author		189

PREFACE TO PART 4

UNPOISONING THE WELL

The idea behind "unpoisoning the well" is that to make diversity work effectively and work for all of us, we need to rise to the challenge of doing the impossible. Just as one cannot pull the cream out of the coffee once it's been stirred in, once a well has been poisoned about the only thing left to do is seal it up and walk away. But too much is at stake for us to walk away and go our separate directions. We need to stay and figure out a way to unpoison the well, and we need to do it together, collectively. Yes, in spite of everything I have discussed throughout this series, I still believe that diversity is an idea worth saving, an ideal worth working toward, and I think with just a bit of effort from all of us, we really can pull off the impossible. In many ways we *have* to pull off the impossible, because the alternatives are either non-existent or hopelessly bleak. The consequences of the failure of diversity in America aren't just limited to American society. They would have a global impact as well, empowering other communities to build up or retreat into enclaves or to lapse into various forms of extremism to keep others out and keep their communities "pure."

Chapter 1 reviews and confirms why passive aspects of diversity do not create an integrated society. Though the focus of this series is on the United States, the first chapter of Part 4 spends considerable time going over international examples to show how the work of diversity in America is actually a template for what are in fact universal and global problems. The burdens of diversity are individual burdens that we all share equally as individuals, and this chapter not only details the work of diversity but shows how we all play an equal part in building a diversity that works for all.

Chapter 2 revisits the central role that law plays in the construction of diversity. Misunderstandings and misplaced hopes about the law have led to misguided activism about diversity and justice. This chapter highlights what the law can and cannot do, and shows how unrealistic expectations of justice and unrealistic demands of the law create frustrations that in turn foment resentment, anger, and further division. In recent years, a number of tragic and high-profile cases, such as the killing of Trayvon Martin, have led some to claim that the entirety of American society and government are both inherently unjust. There's no denying that injustice happens in America, but that doesn't implicate the whole legal system as a complicit agent in the injustice that occurs. The law has a role to play in crafting diversity, but it is not always the role everyone thinks it should play.

Chapter 3 begins to pull together all of the discussions presented so far to show how we need to confront nearly every aspect of diversity as now have it, whether in terms of policy or practice. This is not to argue that we need to confront diversity in the sense of opposing and dismantling it, but rather to confront all of the problems it has created in order to devise solutions. This is an unflinching and difficult chapter, but it is a chapter that nevertheless argues that without confronting nearly everything we think we know or believe about diversity, we will never get a society that works equally and includes everyone.

Chapter 4 offers a number of practical "tests" with which to judge the viability and value of current policies and practices relating to diversity. It also encourages readers to test themselves and their own actions in the cultivation of diversity. How do we know when something is "racist," for instance? Currently we have simplistic definitions, definitions that are contentious and divisive, but with a series of simple tests, we can create a shared standard that allows for constructive dialogue rather than accusations and suspicions.

While much of the earlier discussion has focused on the roots of the problems we now have in relation to diversity, Chapter 4 discusses how to employ effective solutions in everyday, practical situations. Affirmative action, for instance, is one such "solution" currently in circulation, one that remains controversial. Currently the debate over affirmative action is in the form of a yes/no dichotomy—one side argues that it works and we need more of it, the other side argues that it is racist and needs to be abolished. This chapter shows how a better approach would be to design a more effective type of affirmative action, one that rewards a diversity of *understanding* more than a diversity of mere difference. Rather than target specific categories of existence (Black, Latino, etc.) and try to boost numbers, we should reward individuals—through scholarships, employment opportunities, and so on—for the amount of cross-cultural and inter-cultural awareness they have previously engaged in and cultivated.

Chapter 5 focuses on pragmatism and practicality in applying the new ideas of diversity offered throughout this series. There's always the question of "nice idea, but how does it work in practice?" This chapter offers a tentative response to that question by walking through a number of scenarios in areas such as business and education whereby a new approach to diversity opens up entirely new possibilities for breaking down enclaves and bringing different people together in constructive and integrative ways.

The epilog brings the entire series to a close and reiterates the hope that we really can find a way to make diversity work for all of us. Starting with the example of Boston Marathon bomber Dzhokar Tsarnaev and the idea of "homegrown terrorism," the epilog shows how diversity has been poisoned with unrealistic expectations and self-serving demands. To "unpoison the well" in this case means to remove all of the enmity and division and resentment that diversity has hitherto generated and rebuild it anew in a way that allows everyone an equally constructive role in crafting a new diversity.

CHAPTER 1

THE WORK OF DIVERSITY

At this point, it should abundantly clear that diversity is a mess, that it has lost its way, that it has fallen and can't get up, that it has no rigor save for rigor mortis—you get the idea. Things in the world of diversity are bad, and can easily get much, much worse, even as so many putty-for-brains pundits claim we are heading at warp speed into the utopia of a post-racial America. But now we reach the point in the story where we need to figure out what to do to set things right, to rerail the derailed train of diversity, to defenestrate the awful offal and refenestrate—not sure if refenestrate is a word but roll with it—the faceted assets of diversity. The idea should be clear: things have to be made better. The detritus of the old has to be swept away and the new-car smell of the nascent diversity revolution has to be fragrantly and flagrantly sprayed like olfactory graffiti on the nostrils of our collective nose. Anyway, the main point in all of this is something that I stated in the introduction to this series, which is that no one can make diversity better, no one can make diversity deliver on its tremendous promise, other than ourselves. We need to break away from the pundits, break away from the policymakers, and break away from the idea that diversity is someone else's burden and someone else's task. Bob Marley said it best in "Redemption Song": "Emancipate yourselves from mental slavery, none but ourselves can free our minds." When it comes to re-crafting diversity, it's up to us: we're the ones we've been waiting for all along.

The other thing to remember, and this is the part in all of this where things will have to transform quite dramatically from current practice, is that the responsibilities of diversity are responsibilities we bear *individually* and not collectively. Under the current regime of mental turpitude that passes for diversity, the passive act of belonging to one's identity-based group—checking off the box on the list that seems most like you—is all that is required. Self-appointed leaders of each of these groups fight for more things and more benefits for "their people" and then those more things and more benefits are supposed to just magically trickle down to other members of the group. This approach encourages a certain amount of laziness and complacency—all that is required is to belong or to exist in an identity-based box—that spills over even into the civic sphere. Currently, diversity relies upon a strength-in-numbers approach, where census-watching and head-counting somehow translates into the political voice of a community. What we need instead is a strength-of-self approach, an approach that does not reward or encourage passive membership in homogeneous groups but rather one that opens up new possibilities of situating and understanding our*selves* among others.

I have talked a lot about education so far in my varied and various discussions of diversity, but perhaps a better metaphor at this point in the narrative is a tool belt, one filled with the right tools to rebuild and renovate a better sense of diversity. There will always be room for books in that tool belt, but there is so much more that can be of use here and we need to consider all of it. However one chooses to equip their tool belt, the point is that the tools are yours because you took the time to consider them and choose them. Everyone's tool kit should reflect their sense of self, their share of and contribution to diversity. No more handing out Asian tool belts, Latino tool belts, and so on—filled with prefab tool kits chosen by someone else and handed to you so you can identify with others who have the same belt. The passive approach is certainly the easiest, which is what makes it so appealing to so many people, but it is also the most useless. What we need is a switch to the active voice, and that, I will show, is the true work of diversity.

Going forward versus going back
Imagine what it would be like to grow up in a world without mirrors. How would you develop a sense of your identity? Most likely you would take cues from everyone around you, doing as they do, adopting their tastes and their foods, following their social mannerisms, speaking their language, and so on. Suppose this is your life in a place without mirrors and suppose you grow up from birth in a town in China just outside of Beijing. And suppose that growing up all of your peers always teased you—some made fun of you, the people you encountered looked puzzled, and some were outright hostile to you. You didn't mind all of that—people are people, and anywhere you are in the world there will always be petty and mean people. Now suppose as a gift for your twenty-first birthday, a friend of yours returns from a trip and gives you a very exotic present that allows you to finally see who you are. And suppose that after growing up in that environment—speaking Mandarin as your only language, eating only Chinese food, knowing only Chinese movies and shows, having only Chinese friends, growing up in a Chinese household—after all of that, you finally get a glimpse of yourself in this exotic thing called a mirror, only to see that you are black.

In that moment, you would understand many things, most importantly the gap between who you thought you were and who other people perceived you to be. In your world-view, you thought you were Chinese, just as Chinese as everyone around you. Yet now all of those comments and reactions from everyone else made sense, and you suddenly realize that everyone around you always perceived you as something else—as African, as black, as foreign, as anything other than Chinese. This of course is a very hypothetical example, but it is interesting to think about because of one very important question: what would you do next? Would you stay put and live your life as the Chinese person you feel you are? Would you seek out other black people or move to a different country, say in Africa, and become the person you think you were supposed to be? Would you want to be surrounded by people who look just like you?

I've already mentioned in a previous discussion the example of a woman at UC Berkeley who identified as Costa Rican but faced continuous pressure to "be Latina," a label with which she did not identity because "Latino/a" as she saw it on campus meant primarily to be of Mexican heritage. Another student who came to UC Berkeley felt a similar sort of pressure only in the opposite direction: coming from South Africa, he considered himself African and identified as such, and with an American mother, he considered himself African-American. All that would be fine and dandy, except that he was white—in which case he faced continuous pressure to stop calling himself African or African-American. Whites are just whites, apparently, and they certainly can't be African. Then there is this contribution from popular culture, the episode from the well-known classic American sit-com *Seinfeld*, in which a white, Jewish woman from New York is continuously mistaken for a Chinese woman because she changed her last name from Changstein to Chang. Over the phone, as Donna Chang, she offers advice to one of the other characters, George's mother, who believes (based on her name) that she is receiving sage advice based on Chinese cultural wisdom. Yet when they meet in person and she sees that Donna Chang is not Chinese, she becomes agitated and upset and then rejects the advice she had valued hours earlier because Donna Chang is not Chinese.

As I have tried to make clear, diversity as it is currently practiced and promoted encourages us to find a group that is most "like us" and then stick to it. Self-appointed community leaders within these identity-based groups also encourage this approach as it helps to build their power base: they are the ones most likely to be insistent, for instance, that a Costa Rican woman identify herself as Latina. This is because their leadership credentials are further enhanced if they can lay claim to a larger and larger group of followers whose identity-based future is somehow dependent on them. Here, I am arguing that the first step toward a new diversity is to listen less to those self-appointed leaders and listen more to your own sense of who you think you are or who you want to be. Group-oriented identity crafting is based largely on appearance and on place of origin (by birth or by heritage), and so the first positive step we should take is to delink these things and realize that what a person looks like, where they are from, and who they actually are, are all very distinct things that are not inherently or intrinsically linked together.

The other thing we need to do is to come to terms with the idea of "going back." This can mean any one of a number of things: going back "home" (for those who came to their current home country from another country) or going back to one's culture or going back to some part of one's identity (sometimes referred as getting back to our roots). What all of these have in common is that the person in question, the person who has decided to *go back*, has decided to seek the comfort and solace of identity-based homogeneity. In a moment when diversity becomes too much work, such a person decides to embrace homogeneity in a community or location where sameness prevails. Case in point: at a gathering of Filipino-American families where I was present, one of the younger Filipino-Americans stated with concern that he had become "all Americanized." Though he had lived his whole life in America and had taken advantage of all the opportunities that it provided, he felt that being Americanized was a bad thing. At the encouragement of those from "his community," he had decided it was time to go back to the Philippines for a while, and then later return to America, vowing to stay close to his community to retain what he apparently thought his identity was. He wanted to be seen as American, but didn't want to become Americanized.

The problem with this scenario is that becoming "all Americanized" when you live in a place called America should actually be seen as a positive thing. I can't imagine moving to the Philippines and then one day years later saying that I was worried I had become "Filipinized" and so had to take action to stop that from progressing any further. For diversity to work, we have to drop this idea that "going back" is a good thing. Diversity relies upon mutual trust, and it is hard to develop mutual trust when half the people in the room have one foot out the door, just in case things don't go as well as they wanted. Diversity requires us to be all in, both feet firmly planted in the same room, to let go of what we thought was there to go back to, and to go forward and accept the challenges of creating a new identity. So long as we retain a default option that says if a new sense of self proves difficult I can always recede back into my homogeneous community and adopt the prefab identity it provides, there will be no absolute trust, and without absolute trust, there can be no vibrant sense of diversity that works for all of us.

To show why this is the way it has to be, here are two dramatic scenes with four dramatic characters, two that go forward, and two that go back.

A Tale of Two Diversities: A Short Drama in Two Scenes

Scene One: In which our two actors go forward
Anyone with even a passing interest in country music knows that Nashville is the heart and soul of the country music scene. On any

given day in Nashville, there are a dazzling number of shows any visitor can choose from to hear a taste of country, ranging from bigger stadium-type venues to local honky-tonk bars where you can find, as Garth Brooks once famously penned, friends in low places. And while every genre of music has its stereotypes—country music has its cowboys, bluegrass has its mountain boys, rap has its gangstas, rock and roll has its rebels—one person who has bucked the stereotype to transform the face of country music in more ways than one is a certain Hank Sasaki. Now, if you're wondering which part of Tennessee the name Sasaki hails from, you'd be a bit off in your geography. Sasaki is actually a Japanese name, and yes, Hank Sasaki came originally from Japan, from a small rural village in fact. And yet, there came a day in his youth, growing up in Japan some time in the 1980s, when he heard an American country music song—one by Hank Williams, to be specific—and realized that his heart had found its soundtrack. Soon he had himself a guitar, and moved to the relatively big city of Fukuoka on the northern tip of the island of Kyushu in Japan. Fukuoka might have been the big city compared to the village, but it was no match for the paradise of country music, and Hank—not his original first name, in case you are wondering—never gave up on his dream of playing country music in Nashville, Tennessee. And it is there where, if you were lucky enough to be in town when he was giving a show (Hank Sasaki sadly passed away in July 2015), you could find Hank Sasaki playing his country music, alongside a number of other regulars in the Nashville scene, and singing about the things that make country music what it is, as if he were born under a wide Wyoming sky in the middle of a cattle run.

Hank Sasaki is no novelty act, nor is he an impersonator. This is not a scene in Las Vegas, where you become uncomfortably aware of just how many people spend their lives impersonating Elvis and just how many of them do it badly (much as a child feels that first pang of discomfort walking through a shopping mall and seeing eight different Santa Clauses, half of whom emit the faint stench of Jim Beam and Twinkies with every short-winded Ho Ho Ho). No, Hank Sasaki is the real deal. Coming from a society where traditional culture and conformity are highly valued, as they are in Japan, it takes a strong pull of the heart in a different direction to realize that this beautiful music from the heart of America is one's true calling. It takes an even stronger pull to talk the twangy talk and walk the honky-tonk walk all the way to Nashville. Had he simply backed down and stayed "with his own kind," the good people of Nashville would not have had the realization that country comes in all sorts of cultural flavors—just listen to Sasaki's song "I am a Japanese Cowboy"—and the good people of Japan would not have had the realization that culture is not always destiny. There's a big new world out there, and the cultural fetishists and groupthink leaders that dominate the world of diversity right now would want the Hank Sasakis of the world to choke down their moment of self-realization and recede back to the world of group-based conformity. "STOP TRYING TO BE OTHER CULTURES!" they would shout. Yet it is that moment of self-realization, that moment when Hank Sasaki walked the path he wanted to walk and lived the dream he wanted to live, that points to the world that diversity ought to be offering us. And Hank wanted to dream big—he wanted to show the world that country music is truly international, that one can find the cowboy heart in any place from Andorra to Zimbabwe, and not just and only in Nashville. It seems to me that a dream like that can only take things in a good direction.

And now let's switch gears slightly and look at someone who went *to* Japan, rather than come out of it. Martti Turunen grew up in a small village in the eastern part of Finland, living through the violent years of World War II and then living pretty much as any Finnish youth might have lived, that is until he went to Japan in the 1960s at the age of 27 as a Lutheran missionary. Much as Hank Sasaki found the seductive muse of country music calling to him from America, Martti Turunen found the seductive muse of Japanese culture calling to him shortly after he arrived in Japan. So much so, in fact, that Martti Turunen decided he wanted to *become* Japanese, and so one day walked into the Japanese immigration office and stated his desire to become *legally* Japanese, as in, to become a Japanese citizen, much to the consternation of immigration officials in Japan. You see, becoming Japanese was a very difficult thing to do for a foreigner, especially since no one had really tried to do that before. There was no template. Japan was a tight-knit culture, and while we sometimes think that tight-knit cultures are strong cultures, we forget that what it also means is that outsiders are unwelcome and excluded. Martti Turunen thus had to go through a series of rigorous tests to "prove" that he was truly Japanese, tests that immigration officials fully expected him to fail. After all, a foreigner couldn't really be Japanese, could he? So the process of naturalization got started, complete with periodic and random inspections of his lifestyle. Officials would randomly drop by at dinner-time to see if he was having Japanese food and eating with chopsticks, or drop by at bedtime to make sure he was sleeping on a futon and not a Western-style bed. Japanese law requires that all citizens have a Japanese name that can be written in *kanji* (Chinese characters used in Japanese), and so Martti Turunen changed his name to Marutei Tsurunen (Japanese style is Tsurunen Marutei). Having passed all of the tests and having gone through all of the steps one might take to "become Japanese," Martti Turunen legally became Marutei Tsurunen and a Japanese citizen in 1979, settling with his Japanese wife in Yugawaramachi in the prefecture of Kanagawa in eastern Japan, near the city of Yokohama.

For a foreigner to become Japanese was no easy feat, and while many a Japanese person could accept him as a Japanese *citizen*, they found it difficult to accept the idea that he was a Japanese *person*. But Marutei Tsurunen didn't just stop with the transformation of his legal identity. He decided he wanted to get involved in politics, and so he ran for office, first for the local city council in Yugawaramachi in 1992 and then—in spite of continuous death threats from a few livid Japanese people who could not accept this foreigner thinking he could actually be Japanese—in the Japanese Diet (parliament). After losing a few close elections for parliament, he ultimately won a seat as a candidate for the Democratic Party of Japan in 2002 (for which he was re-elected in 2007). He even wrote a book about his experiences—in Japanese—called *Here Comes the Blue-Eyed Assemblyman*, in which he discusses his desire to become Japanese and also his legitimacy in representing other Japanese people. Marutei Tsurunen could have done a lot of different things along the way—he could have sought out the comfort of the Finnish community in Japan or hung out with other Westerners, or he could have just given up and accepted his status as a perpetual foreigner in Japan. But he knew what he wanted to be and paved the way for others like him to find their own identity, no matter how different it might be from what others want you to be or think you should be. Marutei Tsurunen has developed a reputation in Japan as a politician who represents the interests and rights of the marginalized and disenchanted citizens in Japan, and over time has shown other Japanese people that "being Japanese" is a category that can and should be open to anyone who wants to enter.

Note very carefully the actions of Hank Sasaki and Marutei Tsurunen. Both of them understood the values and norms of the cultural environments they wished to join, and voluntarily adopted them and assimilated to them. Yet neither of them lost their identity or even wanted to—Marutei Tsurunen is aware that he is blue-eyed and Japanese at the same time, Hank Sasaki knows he is a true-blue cowboy who also happens to be Japanese—and both understood that there is a certain amount of respect that needs to be shown to one's new environment to join that environment and be accepted within it. What you don't see is Marutei Tsurunen campaigning in Japan that Japanese people should learn Finnish, or that he should be allowed to change his name back to Martti Turunen, or that Japanese people who cannot pronounce his name properly (as it would be in Finnish) are ignorant and racist, or that he should be allowed to conduct his business in Finnish and Japanese people just have to "get over it." You don't see him hanging out with "his people" and advocating for more Finnish things in Japan, and you don't see him complaining that he is becoming "all Japanized" and running back to Finland to be among Finns and drink himself drunk on the elixir of Finnish homogeneity. You also don't see Hank Sasaki demanding that Garth Brooks learn Japanese or that country music should be more Japanese, nor do you see him hanging out with Japanese musicians as "his people" and performing only in Japanese venues. For many diversity advocates and activists in America, both of them would no doubt be seen as "sell-outs" to their community, people who "lost" their culture, but that is precisely where those activists and advocates are so offensively wrong: Marutei Tsurunen and Hank Sasaki are the pioneers of diversity who take us forward, and it is the self-appointed diversity "experts"—the ones who immerse themselves in their own homogenous communities, who demand acceptance without assimilation and platitudes without participation—that are holding us back and holding us down.

Scene Two: In which our two actors go back
Most people who have been to Fiji know it as a so-called island paradise, a place where every view is beautiful, every beach is perfect, and every resident subsists on a diet of coconuts and rum-based cocktails. In the reality-called-and-has-some-different-news-for-you department, however, you might be surprised to hear that Fiji has experienced not one, not two, but three coups since independence in 1970, and all of them have been coups caused entirely by

deeply divisive issues of identity. For anyone who thinks that diversity in America should be easy, I should point out that Fiji's highly dysfunctional identity-based politics is generated by a population that consists almost entirely of two—yes, *two*—identity groups. On the one hand, there are the indigenous Fijians, who as one might expect claim Fiji as their indigenous homeland. On the other, there are the Indo-Fijians, Fijian citizens of Indian descent who came to Fiji starting in the nineteenth century through opportunities created by links to the British Empire (India and Fiji were both British colonies). Though at one point in the 1990s the population percentage of each group seemed to be approaching parity—close to 50% indigenous Fijian with a rapidly-growing Indo-Fijian population at around 44%—the population percentages now, largely as a result of diversity-related issues in Fiji, are approaching indigenous Fijian 60% and Indo-Fijian 40%.

Numbers only tell part of the story, however. Before we meet the main character of this story, I should also explain the nature of the identity-based divisions in Fiji. Fiji is the only place I know of where two diversity-related legal facets of identity come into direct conflict with one another: indigenous rights and minority rights. We normally think of indigenous rights and minority rights as rights against the dominant population group(s), but in Fiji, it is a case of minority rights against the dominant indigenous group and indigenous rights against the minority group. According to the indigenous leaders and politicians, the priority is clear: indigenous rights always trump minority rights. Why? Because the indigenous people of Fiji have only Fiji to call home, they argue, whereas the Indo-Fijians already have India as a homeland and can always "go back" anytime they want. Stereotypes also come into play here. Indo-Fijians dominate the urban-based economy and other forms of trade in Fiji, so most indigenous Fijians see them as materialistic and greedy, people who are in Fiji only to make money to take or send back to India (many indigenous Fijians refer to Indo-Fijians as the "real colonizers" rather than the British). Indo-Fijians of course see themselves as industrious and hard-working, and claim that the indigenous Fijians do not do better economically because they are lazy islanders with more of a love for leisure than for work. Yep, it's ugly.

The three coups that Fiji has endured since independence in 1970—the coups occurred in 1987, 2000, and 2006—have all been coups relating to the tensions between the indigenous Fijians and Indo-Fijians. Indigenous Fijians argue that since Fiji is their only homeland, they cannot afford to lose that homeland to the "immigrant" Indo-Fijians. The indigenous Fijians, they claim, have no place to "go back" to. As a result, there is a persistent belief among many indigenous Fijians that the political system of Fiji should always remain under the control of the dominant indigenous people. Even beyond politics, there is a belief among indigenous Fijians that Indo-Fijians have an obligation to adopt Fijian ways, rather than replicate an Indian lifestyle in Fiji. According to Taufa Vakatale, an indigenous Fijian and former Deputy Prime Minister for Education and Technology, minority rights only exist to help minorities assimilate to the dominant culture, and minorities who do not assimilate and who insist on recreating the cultural environment of their home country in their new host country—and here of course he is referring to the Indo-Fijians—are racists.[1] (And to belabor a point I have made throughout all of these discussions, note how the indigenous Fijian makes it clear that Indo-Fijians—people of color—can be racist.)

The 1987 coup was designed to create a new constitution for Fiji—which was eventually promulgated in 1990—that would ensure indigenous dominance in politics and society. For much of

---

1 Taufa Vakatale, "Multiculturalism vs Indigenous Cultural Rights," in Margaret Wilson and Paul Hunt (eds.), *Culture, Rights, and Cultural Rights: Perspectives from the South Pacific* (2000), 69-81

the early 1990s, however, Fiji came under intense pressure from the United Nations and the Commonwealth countries to create a more inclusive and "multicultural" constitution, which eventually they did—albeit reluctantly. When the first elections were held under the new "multicultural" constitution in May 1999—Fiji has a parliamentary system—a series of political twists and quirks conspired to produce the unthinkable: for the first time in its history, Fiji had an Indo-Fijian prime minister, in the person of Mahendra Chaudhry.

After only one controversial year in office, a group of indigenous Fijians decided it was time to take Mahendra Chaudhry hostage, along with most of the Fijian parliament, and announced a coup to return Fiji to indigenous Fijian rule. Mahendra Chaudhry was quickly removed from office and stripped of his power, and eventually, in July 2000, Chaudhry was released, along with the other hostages, by the leaders of the coup. The long and complex story of what happened in the aftermath of this coup (including another coup that occurred in 2006) is something that need not concern us for this particular example. Instead, I want to focus on what Mahendra Chaudhry did next, after he was released.

After so much political drama, after claims by coup leaders that Indo-Fijians were not "true" Fijians because they were more India-focused than Fiji-focused, after so many claims that having Mahendra Chaudhry as prime minister was like having Fiji being ruled by a foreigner, and after so many claims by Indo-Fijians that none of those claims were true, that Indo-Fijians were completely devoted to Fiji—Mahendra Chaudhry, as soon as he was released, boarded a plane and flew straight to India, where he received a hero's welcome. By "going back" to India without hesitation, when there were so many other safe places to go to, Mahendra Chaudhry ended up giving the impression that the coup leaders actually had a legitimate point, that Indo-Fijians weren't really Fijians at all but rather Indians who lived in Fiji. Mahendra Chaudhry had *gone back* and gone "home." To make matters worse, relatives of Mahendra Chaudhry who still lived in India had met with the then prime minister of India, Atal Beharee Vajpayee, and asked him to use whatever diplomatic powers available to help restore Chaudhry to the position of prime minister in Fiji and also to protect the Indo-Fijian community in Fiji. Whatever intentions were behind all of these maneuvers, the end result was a huge boost of support for the coup leaders among the indigenous Fijian population back in Fiji, who suddenly thought there might be some credibility to the claim that the Indo-Fijian community is more attached to India than to Fiji, more inclined to "go back" to their "real" home than stay put and build a new one in Fiji.

Meanwhile, thousands of miles away in a land called Peru, a whole different sort of political drama was brewing, one with a surprise ending that looks a lot like what happened in Fiji. In 1990, Alberto Fujimori was elected president of Peru. Fujimori had not been the front-runner during the campaign that preceded the election, where other, more high-profile candidates, including novelist Mario Vargas Llosa, grabbed most of the headlines and generated most of the photogenic eye-drivel that for some reason politicians continuously think people want to see. But when the votes were counted, Fujimori's name came out on top and Peru had a new president. Peru at that time was in the midst of a long-running security crisis with the Maoist group *Sendero Luminoso* ("Shining Path") becoming increasingly aggressive and violent in its insurgency. Peru was also in the midst of economic crisis. As a result, Fujimori had to prove his mettle right from the start as someone who was competent and effective at leading the country to better times.

As it turns out, Fujimori was indeed effective at tackling these crises, but effective in a controversial, you-can't-argue-with-results sort of way. Fujimori's economic policies, which became known as Fujishock, were neoliberal economic reforms that promised long-term viability in exchange for short-term misery. His security measures, while successful in slowly eroding the power of Sendero Luminoso, came at the cost of suspending a number of key elements of Peru's democratic institutions through a process known as the *Fujigolpe* (Fujicoup) starting in 1992.

But again, I am less interested in Fujimori's political accomplishments and policies as much as I am in the issue of identity, and that means the moment we should focus on here would be the moment when everything came to an unexpectedly abrupt end for Fujimori. As a result of Fujimori's controversial measures, and regardless of whatever success they may have had or whatever popular support they may have generated, Fujimori came under investigation for a number of his actions, and while he was out of the country in November 2000 attending an economic conference in Brunei, he caught wind of a potential call for his arrest upon his return to Peru. At that point, he decided to *fax* his resignation from the presidency to the Peruvian government (not kidding). But what Fujimori did next is the main part of the plot here: the next thing he did was to board a plane and head straight to Japan. The Peruvian Congress refused to accept his resignation, preferring instead to formally divest him of office on the grounds that he was "permanently morally disabled."

But let's focus on Fujimori's decision to head straight to Japan. Alberto Fujimori was born in Peru of parents who were immigrants from Japan to Peru. As Japanese immigrants to Peru, Fujimori and his family would have been a part of what is called the *chino* community, a name that means "Chinese" but includes pretty much anyone of Asian descent. In Peru, it seems, if you are Korean, Japanese, Taiwanese, or Chinese, you are, well, pretty much just Chinese. To quote the racist cliché, "they all look the same," at least as far as the *Peruanos* (Peruvians) are concerned. When Alberto Fujimori was born, aside from the paperwork required by the Peruvian state authorities for the birth of any Peruvian citizen, Fujimori's parents also took the time to go to the Japanese

Embassy in Lima to register young Alberto's birth in the Japanese registry of births, effectively keeping a foot on Japanese territory, as far as Alberto's identity was concerned. This becomes a central issue in what happens next.

To return to the moment where Alberto Fujimori flew directly to Japan, we have the question of course of why—why fly straight to Japan? The reasons quickly became clear to Peruvian investigators, because when they sought extradition of the now-dismissed president to Peru to face the charges of which he had been accused, Japan notified Peru that they would not extradite a Japanese citizen to stand trial in Peru. But wait, Japanese citizen? Yes, in spite of all the hoops that Marutei Tsurunen had to jump through to prove to very skeptical Japanese immigration officials that a Finnish-born person could be Japanese, for Alberto Fujimori, simply being ethnically Japanese bought him a free pass to immediate citizenship. Never mind that he couldn't speak a word of Japanese and Spanish was his mother tongue—if you look Japanese and your parents say you are Japanese, for instance by registering your birth at the Japanese Embassy, then as far as Japan is concerned, no matter where you live and for how long you have lived there, and no matter what passport you might carry, you are Japanese. Alberto Fujimori, former president of Peru, had decided to "go back" to Japan, leaving a multi-layered wake of frustration and consternation in Peru.

Japan wasted no time in getting Alberto Fujimori set up comfortably, offering him a position at a university and also publishing his side of the story as a memoir, strangely written in Spanish but published first in Japanese as a translation (since Fujimori could not write in Japanese). But many in Peru were flummoxed by all of this, particularly the Japanese members of the *chino* community, who suddenly came under suspicion of really being Japanese citizens masquerading as Peruvian citizens just to take advantage of Peru's resources and opportunities. Several international and

Japanese human rights groups got involved, putting pressure on Japan not to allow Fujimori to retain Japanese citizenship because it would give the impression to countries around the world that their ethnic Japanese populations were really just Japanese citizens living abroad, rather than citizens of their respective countries. Rather disturbingly, Japan seemed to indicate, through their embrace of Fujimori, that such a claim was true, that at the end of the day, all Japanese people, wherever they lived and whatever language they spoke and whatever citizenship they held, really *were* Japanese and Japan really *was* their true homeland.

And……*scene*!

Theatrical reviews: A Tale of Two Diversities
Four characters in two very different scenes about diversity. Now that we've seen the drama, what are we to make of all of this? There is no shortage of other anecdotes to show that these sorts of questions come up in the many ways we situate ourselves among others on an everyday basis. At my local YMCA, for instance, there was an employee at the front desk, and a member of the gym who saw her nametag happened to mention that she had a beautiful name, and then asked where her name was from. The woman responded by saying, "I am Tibetan." Suddenly, another woman, an older Asian woman who was standing nearby and who had overheard the conversation, became very agitated, and for some reason felt obligated to intercede. What she said, quite loudly and with great agitation, was this: "Why do you say you are Tibetan? You are Chinese! Say you are Chinese!" The Tibetan woman wanted to take advantage of the freedom in America to practice and proclaim without fear that her identity was Tibetan. But the other woman, who was originally from China, wanted the frame of reference to "go back" to

China, as if the concerns of Chinese identity in America should be viewed with Chinese priorities rather than American ones. The Tibetan woman was clearly distressed by this, but made the decision to let things go rather than escalate an argument that showed no signs of going anywhere constructive.

In another instance, at a screening of a BBC documentary on the targeting of ethnic Tamil civilians by government forces during Sri Lanka's twenty-six year civil war (1983-2009), students of Sri Lankan descent—none of whom were ethnic Tamil—showed up at the event, held on UC Berkeley's campus, to demand that the screening be cancelled, or that they at least be allowed to show their own documentary that showed how all of the charges were fabricated and how the BBC documentary was just "pro-terrorist propaganda." Once again, we have a situation where a group of people living and studying in America wanted to maintain a frame of reference that is determined by "going back," in this case to Sri Lanka.

Then there are the moments when persons who come to the United States and encounter difficulties decide almost as an instinctive reaction that "going back" is the best response. In the infamous case of the 54-million-dollar pants, in which Roy Pearson (a judge, incidentally) sued the owners of a dry-cleaning business for $54 million because they allegedly had ruined his favorite pants, the owners, who were Korean immigrants, decided that "going back" to South Korea was perhaps the best choice of action. Fortunately they decided to stay, and a legal fund was raised for them, though their lawyer, Christopher Manning, ultimately worked on the case *pro bono* (as in, without accepting a fee). As messed up as the case was, the Korean couple ultimately won the case and it has now become a symbol of the need for legal reform against frivolous and outrageous lawsuits.

And what of the position of Japan on the "real" identity of Alberto Fujimori? As strange as it may seem, similar positions by countries that simply cannot let go of their former citizens and their descendants are quite common. There appears to be a tremendous amount of separation anxiety among many countries and many peoples in the world, something that actually frustrates the possibility of achieving diversity in America, or in any other country where significant immigrant populations exist. Part of the work of diversity is that individuals need to make a choice not to think in terms of "going back," and the countries from which they came need to think in terms of "letting go."

To conclude this part of the discussion, I would like to return to a point from the Tale of Two Diversities, which is this interesting little label of identity called *chino*. I mentioned this in relation to Alberto Fujimori in Peru, who hails from the *chino* community, and I mentioned how utterly strange it is that in Peru, the word *chino*, which literally means Chinese, is used when people really mean Asian. Given the cultural differences among and deep divides between persons from China, Japan, and Korea, it seems rather offensive if not forthright racist to simply lump them all together as "Chinese." If you can imagine how much anger would be generated in America, for instance, if someone were to say they were Korean-American and you responded by saying, "meh, Korean, Japanese, Chinese—they're all the same, no difference—just Chinese," you can understand how distortive the label of *chino* is. Yet in the highly dysfunctional world of diversity we have in America, this issue is never really brought to the surface, because even though most Latinos use this word (the world *chino* is used throughout Latin America and even among Latinos in the United States), to admit its use would be to admit that racism could exist among communities of color, something that is always kept out of discussions of diversity in America. I even had a discussion with a visiting scholar from Argentina who tried to explain to me that the use of the word *chino* was not racist because Argentinians did not see anything wrong with it. It's pretzel logic at its finest: imagine someone in America using the N-word and saying it isn't racist as long as she or he doesn't see anything wrong with it. And besides, how difficult is it to use separate words for separate identities? The words *chino* (Chinese), *coreano* (Korean), and *japonés* (Japanese) all exist in Spanish, so maybe it's time to spend a little less time trying to claim that Latinos can't be racist and a little more time asking Latinos to use less-racist language.

Bangkok Dangerous: Why culture is not who you are
It's hard to say what the bigger force of attraction is in being susceptible to the idea of "going back"—national identity or cultural identity—but so long as it is there it will always act as a brake in the process of self-determination (in this case, of the individual self), or, as I discussed earlier, as a set of training wheels that permanently reduces one's identity to a child-like state. And of course, one might ask whether an American who stays in America is somehow in a similarly stunted position in terms of their identity, but this is where America the Improbable comes back into action. American diversity is a unique experiment, based on the revolutionary premise that people can come from pretty much any different walk of life and somehow learn to walk together in harmony. This is why it is so important to get diversity right in America, because if it fails, it will send a message loud and clear to the rest of the world to stop trying. It would tell people everywhere to stick to their own kind, to aim for homogeneity rather than diversity. I will admit that there are plenty of Americans who are genuinely stunted in their sense of identity, either because they have opted for the lazy pre-fab approach of finding their "people" and imitating a culture they believe to be their own, or because they have opted just for sheer laziness and never tried to figure out who they actually are. One of the things about American democracy is that it lets you be whatever you want to be, even if the thing you want to be is stupid.

It seems to me that if you enter into American society and want it to work as a cohesive *and* diverse culture, then you at least need to accept the challenge that diversity proposes: to use the freedom offered to you to create a sense of self that is truly your own. It is one thing to use your cultural identity as a starting point, a launch vehicle of sorts, and quite another to treat your cultural identity as the final point of arrival, as the definitive statement of who you are. To do the latter is a bit like buying a new computer with ten thousand different ways to customize it to your tastes, but then shying away from the options and just using the pre-set default options. It's the option for people who don't want to think for themselves, and neither diversity nor democracy work well when people do not think for themselves. There are many other reasons why treating one's cultural background as the definitive statement of who you are—think of this the next time you see a T-shirt that says "Filipino pride" or "Korean pride," or just consider a T-shirt that you hope you never see but would be equally as useless, "White pride" (and think about why we should be equally offended by all three but somehow aren't)—but here is one glaring example of why an excessive reliance on cultural background is a hopelessly flawed approach that works against the interests of diversity.

About every ten years or so, the United Nations hosts a global conference on human rights that is designed to survey the progress of the past decade and to map out areas where more work needs to be done. Now I will admit that the United Nations tends to approach the problems of the world with all the power and pragmatism of a plastic spork at a knife fight, but for this example, let's just assume that a plastic spork is a good and useful thing. In 1993, the global conference on the state of human rights in the world was to be held in Vienna, Austria. The conference was indeed held in Vienna, but the Vienna conference is not the conference that is most significant for the point I am making here. In the months leading up to the Vienna conference, there was another conference held in Bangkok, Thailand, convened by several Asian nations who had decided to take a collective stand against the very idea of global human rights, and the giant tool they were going to use to do this was "Asian culture." In essence, the conference in Bangkok was designed to create a collective cultural stance against the idea and practice of universal human rights on the grounds that human rights were really just "Western" ideas. If Asian countries adopted them, it would require Asian cultures to adopt the values of Western countries, which would amount to the destruction of Asian culture. Asian cultures therefore had to resist human rights, or at least assert a right to reinterpret them based on Asian cultural values, in order to save and preserve Asian culture from this alleged Trojan Horse of Western values called human rights.

The Bangkok Conference of 1993 did eventually cook up a few general principles that those in attendance claimed represented the essence of Asian culture. Among them were (1) an acceptance of hierarchy (so the egalitarian elements of human rights could be rejected); (2) a respect for authority (so democratic elements of human rights could be rejected); and (3) a respect for cultural diversity (so anything that seemed "Western" in human rights could be rejected as culturally inappropriate for Asian countries). Collectively, these ideas amounted to what was called the "Asian Values" challenge to human rights, and the goal of the Bangkok Conference was to create a unified voice for Asian countries to stand against the "Western ideas" that they claimed would dominate the Vienna Conference, which was to be held a few months later.[2]

In reality, however, what the Bangkok Conference ended up doing is showing why culture is a fragile, diffident, and often

---

2 Much has been written on the "Asian Values" challenge to human rights. For a quick overview, see "The Rise of Asian Values" at http://therightsfuture.com/common-tracks/asian-values/

incoherent basis for identity, something that is as true for countries as it is for individuals. To paraphrase Elizabeth Barrett Browning: "O Culture, how do I question thee? Let me count the ways." First of all, not all of the countries in Asia attended the conference. While China and Malaysia decided Asian culture trumped human rights and "Western style" democracy, so as to give Asian cultures considerable leeway in watering down and manipulating human rights for politically convenient ends, other countries such as Japan and South Korea reached the conclusions that (1) they were completely Asian, (2) they were highly supportive of human rights, and (3) democracy was a very good thing indeed. In other words, Asian countries couldn't agree on what it meant to be Asian. So rule number one in the world of culture: if you are going to invoke it, you need to be completely consistent. On this first point, the Bangkok Conference failed.

On to point number two. The countries that attended the Bangkok Conference and who supported the idea of Asian Values were not even consistent with their own Asian cultural values, as they themselves defined them. Let's take a look at the views of Mahathir Mohamed, the prime minister of Malaysia at the time and one of the chief proponents of the Asian Values challenge. According to Mahathir, Asian cultures respect authority and so are not naturally or culturally amendable to the egalitarian and democratic values that are prominent in Western cultures (which is a hard argument to make anyway, given that most of the history of Western culture is decidedly non-egalitarian and non-democratic). Now, if that were true, and people in Asian cultures respected authority and power and therefore were not interested in the egalitarian rights of democracy, including the right to oppose authority, then we arrive at a rather embarrassing contradiction.

Clearly, a Western country like America was far more powerful than Malaysia was in 1993, so if Mahathir were true to his own cultural ideals, he would not have been trying to oppose a more powerful country like America and would have instead shown deference and followed the wishes of the more powerful countries at the conference in Vienna. Asian citizens with Asian values were supposed to defer to their leaders, so it stands to reason that if Malaysia actually had Asian values, it would also defer to more powerful countries at the United Nations. That, according to Mahathir, was what a proper Asian would do. And yet there he was, striving for egalitarianism and democracy ahead of the Vienna conference, trying to give Malaysia an equal voice to the West, even as he denied that equal voice to anyone who questioned his style of rule in Malaysia. Based on this glaring and rather embarrassing contradiction, we can say that on this second point, the Bangkok conference failed.

How about a third point as well? Why, certainly. The last point I will mention in relation to this attempt to concoct a top-down version of "authentic" (oh, how I despise that word) Asian culture is the fact that there was a second conference held in Bangkok in 1993, a shadow conference of Asian non-governmental organizations (NGOs). These NGOs were from the very same countries that were pontificating about how Asian culture did not need or want the egalitarian and democratic values embedded in human rights by the oh-so-sinister West, and they had a message for their own political and cultural representatives who claimed to speak on behalf of Asia and its values, namely: (1) we are very Asian and (2) we want human rights and democracy. So the question is, when we have two Asian cultural voices saying the opposite things at the same time, which one represents Asia? Who legitimately speaks for Asian culture, and must there be only one voice for Asian culture to be authentic?

I am asking these questions about Asian culture for now, but they apply equally well for any culture that claims to be, well, a culture. If the Asian countries at the Bangkok Conference are right, and Asian culture is not compatible with egalitarian ethics and democratic values, then Asian-American groups asking for more rights and equality in the United States must have lost the Asian part of their identity. After all, the countries that supported the Asian Values challenge claimed that all of those Asian NGOs that offered an alternative point of view—that one could be Asian and also support democracy and human rights—had been corrupted and tainted by foreign and Western values, and could not truly call themselves Asian. Myanmar, for instance, had (at least until 2010) continuously tried to discredit the pro-democracy activism of Aung San Suu Kyi by claiming she was merely a mouthpiece of Western values, going so far as to claim she was proposing the "re-colonization" of Myanmar by Britain. Aung San Suu Kyi's husband, Michael Aris, was British, and the official Burmese press was fond of referring to her as "Mrs. Michael Aris" to call attention to her alleged foreign affinities. Fortunately, with the advent of a partial democratic transition in Myanmar in 2010, the quality of discourse has gone up, though the new constitution of Myanmar still makes it impossible for Aung San Suu Kyi to become president because members of her family (including her children) hold non-Burmese citizenship and thus retain "foreign loyalties."

Even then, there are tremendous inconsistencies in the ways that Asian countries themselves represent Asian culture, even in those countries that support the idea of a reinterpretation of human rights based on Asian values. China and Singapore both claim that in Asian culture, the family comes first and the individual comes second, so human rights principles that protect individual rights are incompatible with Asian culture. This of course is part of the stereotype that for Asians, "family is important," while apparently for Westerners, the family is meaningless. But if Asian cultures put the family first, then why did Singapore have to create an official set of "Shared Values" for all Singaporeans, values that include a reminder that the group comes before the individual, and why does the government spend so much time and money promoting those values (unsuccessfully, I might add)? Shouldn't Singaporean citizens, as Asians, already have those values? And if family comes first for Asians, why did China have to pass a law in July 2013 requiring Chinese citizens to visit their parents?[3] If a government has to spend so much time and energy and money to tell Asians how to be Asian, then we can only reach one conclusion in all of this: being Asian means too many different things to be a rational foundation for a person's identity. At best, it can only be a small part, a place to start, a set of training wheels. What that means for diversity in America is that all of the current emphasis on finding a group that is "you"—whether cultural, racial, ethnic, or religious, or any other standard identity category—and then using that pre-fab identity as a way to express your "authentic" self and advocate for rights and privileges accordingly is a highly imperfect if not entirely useless way to orchestrate diversity. It's time to take the training wheels off and start exploring the possibilities of all the other things that we can be.

Bangkok Dangerous: The Sequel
Incidentally, there have been some interesting revisions to the situation I discussed earlier regarding the "Asian values" challenge to human rights, especially within Malaysia. Before I say what they are, let me remind you, dear reader, why a discussion of Malaysia might show up in a book on diversity in America. The short answer is this: too many commentators and critics on diversity in America have no substantive experience outside of America with which to compare the American experience. I think a comparative perspective adds a necessary dimension to the debate that has been sorely missing for so many years, as this example from Malaysia will show.

I mentioned that Malaysian prime minister Mahathir Mohamad was one of the chief architects of the Asian values challenge to

---

3 Celia Hatton, "New China law says children 'must visit parents'," *BBC News* (July 1, 2013) at http://www.bbc.com/news/world-asia-china-23124345

human rights, which as a reminder, was the challenge that human rights and associated freedoms were really "Western" ideas that were culturally inappropriate for Asian countries like Malaysia. I should also add that he was joined in this effort to push back against "the West" by then deputy prime minister Anwar Ibrahim. The whole "Asian values" project started in the early 1990s, and within Malaysia, Mahathir and Anwar Ibrahim were the most vocal proponents of this challenge.

In 1997, however, a massive financial crisis hit the region. The financial crisis started in Thailand in July but spread quickly to the rest of Asia, hitting several other countries, including Malaysia. The crisis spread so rapidly largely due to networks of corruption that revealed large holes in the financial infrastructure of many countries in Asia. Though Malaysia's economy was strong enough to weather the crisis relatively well, there was a public spat over the causes of the economic damage between the prime minister (Mahathir) and the deputy prime minister (Anwar Ibrahim). Remember that one of the elements that supposedly defined Asian culture, according to the Asian values approach, was that Asians respected hierarchy and authority. So when the deputy prime minister openly defied the prime minister by offering an alternative opinion, Mahathir decided that Anwar Ibrahim had to be taught a lesson.

Starting in 1999, Anwar Ibrahim was fired from his post and expelled from his party, and was eventually jailed on charges of sodomy and homosexuality (which are illegal in Malaysia). The rift between Mahathir and Anwar Ibrahim and the consequences it set in motion are still a central part of Malaysian politics even as I write here in 2017. For my purposes, I only want to detail two very important changes that occurred as a result of the political rift.

First, Anwar Ibrahim underwent a change of perspective on things as he sat in a jail cell on what definitely appeared to be very trumped up charges. It turns out when you are thrown in jail like that, with little recourse to justice, human rights start sounding pretty attractive. Whether they are Western or not doesn't really matter. What matters is if they help provide justice. Anwar Ibrahim was eventually released from prison a few years later (though he is, as of this writing, back in jail, under the same charges) and after his release he set about creating a new political party, the Parti Keadilan Rakyat (PKR), or the People's Justice Party. The platform of the PKR strongly endorses both democratic freedoms and human rights, the very things that Anwar Ibrahim had stood against just a few years previously, all on the grounds of Asian culture.

Anwar Ibrahim's political party was the first political party in Malaysia since independence in 1957 to openly endorse democracy and human rights (though Malaysia has been a democracy since independence). It was also the first party to do something else, but before you can understand the importance of this other thing, I have to describe briefly Malaysia's approach to diversity. Malaysia has three main population groups, all of which are technically ethnic groups though in Malaysia they are usually referred to as racial groups. Those three ethnic groups are Malay, Indian, and Chinese. If you are one of the proponents of our current version of diversity in America right now, you're probably thinking that Malaysia must be utopia—only three ethnic groups, and all of them consist of people of color. The reality, however, is that ethnic tensions and strained race-relations have dominated Malaysian politics since 1957.

The approach that Malaysia settled on right after independence was to keep the three identity groups separate. The party that has ruled Malaysia since 1957, the United Malays National Organization (UMNO), has always promoted the interests of the ethnic Malay population on the grounds that, while Indians could always "go back" to India, and Chinese could always "go back" to China, ethnic Malays had nowhere to "go back" to, and thus had to be protected through special rights and privileges not available to the Indian and Chinese populations. (On a side note, I'd like to point out that "Indian" is neither an ethnicity nor a race, and in Malaysia, if your heritage is from, say, Sri Lanka, it doesn't matter. You're just "Indian." Compare that to Peru's use of the word *chino* (Chinese) to refer to anyone from Asia.)

Both Mahathir and Anwar Ibrahim, I should point out, were originally in UMNO. When Anwar Ibrahim created his new political party, however—and here is the *second* big change in Malaysian politics—the PKR also became the first political party to openly endorse a multiethnic platform. Previously Malaysian citizens supported parties based primarily on ethnicity or race. The PKR welcomed all three groups to join, rejecting separation and promoting integration. Anwar Ibrahim's message attracted support quickly, so much so that it seemed to be the first party since independence in 1957 that could directly challenge the dominance of UMNO. So real was the threat from Anwar Ibrahim that the ruling party overturned his acquittal, reinstated the charges against him (sodomy and homosexuality), and threw him back in jail so he couldn't stand for election.

As for Mahathir, who stepped down as prime minister in 2003, he has recently undergone a surprising transformation of his own. After spending years in quiet political retirement, he has re-emerged on the political scene, this time openly supporting the very ideals he previously denounced. Not only did he personally lend his support to activist-group *Bersih* in November 2016 (Bersih, which means "clean" in Malay, promotes free and fair democratic elections), but also, when by sheer accident he met Anwar Ibrahim in court in September 2016, the two rivals shook hands and issued a joint statement criticizing the current prime minister (Najib Razak, from UMNO) and promoting democratic rights and freedoms for all Malaysians.

What lessons does all this give us for diversity in America? Let's make a list. (1) Culture isn't the ultimate arbiter of anything, and culture can change. (2) People can overcome cultural values and change their perspective. (3) A person's cultural perspective is most likely to change and change for the better through interaction with different groups of people with different experiences. (4) Whether human rights and democracy are Western is irrelevant—Anwar Ibrahim "appropriated" them and he did not become less Malaysian as a result. (5) Separating ethnic and racial groups is a disaster for diversity.

I would like to emphasize the last point. In a later chapter I am going to discuss a rising trend in the American version of diversity, namely the creation of "safe spaces," places where minority groups can retreat to be among their own kind. If the experience of Malaysia tells us anything, it is that these "safe spaces" are a disaster for both diversity and democracy.

The language of diversity
Language shows up in discussions of diversity in a variety of different ways, some expected and obvious, and some unexpected and less obvious. Think, for instance, of the word "gypsy." Most people use it unthinkingly, and a good number of American pop songs have some kind of gypsy theme to them—for example, Stevie Nicks' well-known tune "Gypsy," which has it right there in the title. But the word gypsy, believe it or not, is a racial slur (don't think Stevie Nicks knew that), since it is a short colloquialization for Egyptian, from where people mistakenly assumed Gypsies, more correctly known as Roma, came from. So, too, is another word derived from the word gypsy, namely the verb "to gyp" (also "to gip") which means to treat someone like a gypsy would presumably treat someone, meaning to cheat or to swindle them. So the next time you go to the store and complain to the manager that you were gipped, think of how racism is sometimes embedded in the very words we choose.

Incidentally, Michelle Obama used the g-word ("gipped") in June 2014 during an interview with ABC-news reporter Robin

Roberts.[4] The reference here is not meant as a claim that Michelle Obama is racist, but rather to show how easily racially-charged language is deployed in our vocabulary. Still, there is a pause-for-reflection moment here. An African-American First Lady uses a racial slur in an interview with an African-American reporter who also came out as lesbian in December 2013. Yet neither of them thought twice about it, most likely because, as I hope I have made clear by now, the slur does not involve either African-American identity or lesbian identity, and so both were probably unaware of issues that involved "other people" from "other communities." The Roma community, on the other hand, thought many times about it, and the Roma blogosphere lit up with complaints and protests after the interview was aired. Once again, this shows why we need to make diversity focus on understanding others and *not* on promoting ourselves.

The language of identity is a very sensitive topic in the United States, and it is one of the main reasons why talking about diversity in America is so awkward and unproductive. Everyone is afraid of offending someone else, wittingly or unwittingly, and being forced to bear the scarlet R of Racism. I know there are many who think this is a peculiarity of American language, that it is somehow evidence of just how racist America is, but it turns out that this is also a universal phenomenon. And actually, what makes America exceptional is the lengths to which we go to try to change our language to fit our different sensibilities about each other. One could travel the world and compile a very disturbing dictionary of negative and unflattering words that most people have about other people. I have already mentioned the word *chino*, the Spanish word that turns all Asians into Chinese people, whether they want

---

4 Jenn Selby, "Michelle Obama criticized for allegedly using racial slur," *The Independent* (June 26, 2014) at http://www.independent.co.uk/news/people/michelle-obama-criticised-for-allegedly-using-racial-slur-9564050.html

to be *chino* or not. Among the Maori of New Zealand, the word Maori means "the people" (same meaning as Inuit among the Inuit people), so apparently the non-Maori are not quite people, and in fact the Maori word *pakeha* refers to white non-Maori, with the understanding that Maori cannot become pakeha and pakeha cannot become Maori. In Hawai'i, among native Hawai'ians, the word *haole* does much the same thing: it renders non-native people into permanent outsiders. In Thailand, the word *khaek* is a slur for people of Indian origin, and refers to the way they supposedly smell. In Burma, the word *kalar* is a racial slur referring to foreigners, especially dark-skinned ones. That's just a few examples—I am quite sure if anyone cared to compile such a dictionary, it would be a lamentably thick tome indeed. It seems that no matter where you go, people have a word to let you know that you don't belong and never will.

Sometimes a single word can be a revolution. In Thakazhi Sivashankarapillai's Malayalam-language novel *Thottiyude Mahan* (Scavenger's Son, 1947), the father of a Dalit (untouchable) family in southern India decides to give his new-born son a name that is traditionally reserved for those of higher status. The name he gives is Mohan, which means prince and reflects high and noble and inherited status. People of higher status are shocked and outraged—how dare a low-life child take on a high-life name? But the father stands his ground and the child grows up to fight against the whole system of inherited (caste) status in India.

But now, let's bring this all back to the United States and look at a new language trend that is developing in the name of diversity: the call for a change to a multi-lingual America. I don't think Americans appreciate how complex the American linguistic landscape is sometimes, and I mean appreciate as in marvel at—between the family names of US citizens and the place names of various American cities, we have so many languages in circulation that it is truly mind-boggling. Not surprisingly, many of those names get a little altered in their pronunciation as different languages interact with the sounds of each of these words. Berkeley, for instance, is in its British origins actually pronounced more like "Barkley", and it is just up the road from a place Vallejo, which in its original Spanish would be pronounced va-ye-ho but in America gets the hybrid treatment of va-le-yo. The process of transition in the pronunciation of these words is the product of a wonderfully complex linguistic diversity.

Nevertheless, there has been a growing trend in recent years to reverse this and revert instead to what might be called the re-nativization of these words. What I mean by that is over the past few decades, there has been a growing movement of "activism" that claims that the mispronunciation of these words (that is, in relation to how they should be pronounced in the native language from which they originate) is yet another instance of racism in America. Since the dominant group in America is assumed to be white and English-speaking, the idea is that something like va-le-yo represents the linguistic oppression of Spanish speakers by the dominant English-speaking group. For these mental munchkins, demanding a return to va-ye-ho (just for starters) is an act of social justice that is part of the struggle for diversity. Every word should be pronounced as it is in its native language, and the linguistic hegemony of English, as the language of the white elite, has to be stopped. Once that happens, they believe, we get more diversity.

There's some genuinely odious reasoning (or lack of reasoning) in this. To utilize an English colloquialism—it's stupid somethin' fierce. To explain why this is so, let's look at names. Way back in 1988, popular singer Gloria Estefan released a statement explaining the "correct" pronunciation of her name. The singer, who is of Cuban descent, has a name that in its Anglicized pronunciation is ES-te-fan (with the stress on the first syllable). The statement she released, however, stated that the "correct" pronunciation is es-TE-fan, with the stress on the second syllable. I hear similar complaints on campus from Hispanics and Latinos about how "stupid" Americans (again, assumed to be white) continuously "butcher" (mispronounce) their names. Many of them see it as a form of racism, an attack on the identity of those with Hispanic heritage, because it forces them to assimilate, through their names, to the white, English-speaking majority of America.

One of the things I love to do when these issues come up is introduce people to my hypothetical Chinese friend, Cuo Cai. How do you pronounce *his* name? I ask. Most people stumble: Koo-oh Kay? Kwo Ka-yee? Some of them try to insert a Chinese accent that really just makes the whole thing embarrassing and offensive. I then tell them that in Mandarin the "c" is pronounced like "ts" so the pronunciation is actually "ts-wo tsa-yee." I can push the issue a bit further at this point and ask a different question. If the person who mispronounced Cuo Cai's name was Latina, then would Cuo Cai be a victim of Latina racism? You might think it is wrong to expect a Latina to know how to pronounce a Chinese name, but it is no more wrong than it is for a Latina to expect a white person to know how to pronounce a Spanish name. With diversity, what we expect from one person we need to expect from all.

I actually don't need to invent a hypothetical Chinese friend to make this point. I can just use my own name. Zook, for instance, has Swiss-German roots, and is correctly pronounced "tsook" (and rhymes with *spook*). The Americanization of the name has made it Zook (rhymes with *book*), with a soft English "z". So the first question is, do I care about the change in pronunciation? No, I don't. *Should* I care about the change? No, I shouldn't. And here's why.

Suppose I am speaking with a group of native Korean speakers—whether or not they are American is irrelevant, but for this illustration, let's say they are American citizens whose first language was Korean. If I introduce myself to them, say, as Professor Zook, many of them will chuckle. They will chuckle because there is no "z" sound in Korean, and so a "j" sound is automatically substituted, and when that happens my name becomes "juk," which in Korean means rice porridge. They chuckle because having a name that means rice porridge is just absurdly silly, sort of like meeting a white American whose family name is Tatertots. I also have a Chinese name written with Chinese characters, since straightforward English names written in the Roman alphabet make little sense in a character-based language. My Chinese name is Zōu Dá Rén (邹达仁). Is it close? Sort of. But again, do I care? Not at all. I understand the whole point of an accent, of the challenge of pronouncing words from other languages, because the whole point of diversity is *to understand ourselves among others.*

Now, if I follow the lead of these so-called diversity activists who think for instance that all Spanish names have to be pronounced as they are in Spanish, I could then say this: "Hey, all you Mandarin and Korean speakers, stop making me a victim of racism and oppression and learn to pronounce my name exactly as it is pronounced in America! Stop having an accent and stop trying to make me assimilate to your Asian ways! I am a victim of your brutality no more!" But if I did that, I wouldn't be an activist. I would be an idiot. And if I were an idiot, I would be like those who think that all Spanish names and words must always be pronounced as a native Spanish speaker would pronounce them—otherwise, it's racist.

What makes me suspicious about these calls for a multilingual America, voiced as they are under the guise of increasing diversity, is that they are done under the current regime of diversity, where we are rewarded for promoting ourselves and not (as it should be) for understanding others. In other words, these calls for a multilingual America are not calls asking Americans to speak more languages, but instead are calls asking other Americans to learn to accept "my" language while "they" don't bother to learn yours. That's not diversity. That's narcissistic laziness with a touch of braindeath thrown in for enhanced intellectual ambience. Think about it, who is making the calls for everyone to learn how to pronounce Spanish names like a native speaker of Spanish? It's the Spanish-speaking communities. But if their call were genuine, they should also be at home learning how to pronounce Vietnamese names in proper Vietnamese, Irish names in proper Irish, or Mandarin names in proper Mandarin, or Tamil names in proper Tamil, or Amharic names in proper Amharic. Similarly, why is it that if Zook is pronounced with Spanish-language sounds, it is referred to as a Spanish accent, but if someone pronounces a Spanish name with English sounds, it is not referred to as an English accent, but rather as an act of "ignorance" by one more imperialist fascist racist who is forcing the whole world to assimilate to the dominant culture in a sinister plot that would make Hitler green with envy. Clearly, this is a misguided plan. If you are keeping score, it looks like this: Stupidity 1, Diversity 0.

More languages, more diversity?
More recently, we have calls to move beyond just pronunciation and move towards adding new languages—officially—to America, beyond English, that is. In 2015, Latinos officially became the majority population in California, and there are more and more calls for recognizing Spanish as an official language in California, again and not surprisingly, from the Latino and other Spanish-speaking communities.[5] Actress Eva Longoria has even become a public advocate of this idea, proclaiming her pride in being Latina and telling America it needs to speak more than one language, by which she means Spanish. The idea here is that an America that only speaks or only wants to speak English is racist and

---

5 See, for example, Roque Planas, "Why the Spanish Language Isn't "Foreign" in the United States," *Huffington Post* (May 27, 2016) at https://www.huffingtonpost.com/entry/why-the-spanish-language-isnt-foreign-in-the-united-states_us_5746fac3e4b055bb11714a36

xenophobic, so we need to learn to be comfortable with many different languages being spoken in America. The problem with this is that it is still a narcissistic "me only" approach, where a diverse America consists of Spanish-speakers speaking Spanish with each other, Arabic speakers speaking Arabic with each other, and so on, so that America becomes a bunch of separate conversations in different languages. Our role is to step back and listen to the foreign sounds we cannot understand and simply admire the diversity of what we hear. Whether we understand each other is irrelevant. What this is really promoting is the formation of *linguistic enclaves*.

With our current (mis)understanding of diversity, where we promote our own identities, some people actually consider this a good idea. But how can we learn to understand one another if we all speak separate languages? If we look at diversity differently, and we see the work of diversity as the enterprise of understanding others, rather than promoting ourselves, we would have something quite different. We would have Spanish speakers learning Arabic, Arabic speakers learning Spanish, Amharic speakers learning Tamil, and Tamil speakers learning Xhosa, and in the middle of it all, *everyone* would be learning English. Until we get to that point, it's all just self-serving gibberish that gives us more division and more racism, and not the thing we want and need, which is more and better diversity.

The problem here is the general sentiment that self-projection and self-promotion is somehow interpreted as an act of enhancing diversity (which it isn't). And this trend is just one part of a larger cascade of proposed "innovations" that have become more and more visible, especially in California. One of these innovations, for instance, is the growing use of Spanish—*without* English subtitles or corresponding English text to explain them—in advertising and in other public places. The idea is that since we have a growing Latino population, we should expect Spanish to be a more prominent part of public life. I myself know Spanish, so I'm not one of those who feels "threatened" by a language other than English.

But I still think it is a serious mistake to accommodate the desires of separate communities to speak separate languages, something that actually works *against* diversity and not *for* it.

I went to the movies not that long ago—yes, at the theater (some people still do that)—and while waiting for the movie to start the theater was showing all sorts of previews, as of course they always do. When the preview for *Machete 2* came on, I noticed that the first part of the preview was a clip of actor Danny Trejo introducing the film in Spanish, without any English subtitles. There are two reasons I can think of why this would be done: one, to introduce the film in Spanish as if to say, if you do not understand what I am saying you need to learn Spanish because it is the wave of the future of America; or two, to appeal to Latino, Hispanic, and other Spanish-speaking audiences to try to cash in on the ethnic ticket, as if to say, If you can understand what I am saying then you should pay to see this film. It could be one or both of those reasons, and regardless of which it is, they are both the wrong approach to achieve a meaningful diversity for America.

Being a professor-type, I do have the luxury of bringing these types of incidents into the classroom for discussion, one of the many things I love about what I do for a living. So I brought this moment into my class to ask my students what they thought of it, and the answers I got were interesting if not surprising. First of all, the only students who thought it was a good thing were the Latino students. For them, it was a moment of pride and visibility. Many other students felt it was a big turn-off, with a few even calling it racist, and said they would not want to see a film that seemed targeted only at Latinos. They felt excluded. To that sentiment, several Latino students responded by saying that the feeling of being excluded was the whole point. One of them even said, "now you know how it feels to be Latino in America." If his point was that by making others feel linguistically excluded, Latinos were somehow turning the tables on their alleged oppressors, I have to point out that this would *not* be an act of diversity, but rather an act of retaliation or vengeance. Keep in mind also that many of the students who said they felt excluded from the film were not white—they were Asian-American, Asian, African-American, and one Ukrainian (a white, non-native English speaker). The thing is, if this is what passes for diversity activism, we should at least be consistent: Japanese-American directors should introduce films in Japanese without subtitles, Chinese-American directors should introduce films in Mandarin or Cantonese (or Taiwanese) without subtitles, German-American directors in German without subtitles, and so on, and when anyone complains that they could not understand what these films were about, we can call them racist for not knowing every other language spoken in America except their own.

English as the one but not the only
So, what am I getting at here? I agree that America is and should be a multilingual country. In many ways, it always has been. I also understand that much of the impetus behind demanding an America that is English-*only* comes usually from people who know nothing about any other languages in the world and have no interest in learning them, They feel threatened by the existence of other, non-English languages in America. That kind of knee-jerk reaction is palpably a form of xenophobia, a fear of what is foreign and different. This is why, as I said much earlier, I do not support the idea of an English-*only* America or any variant thereof, including the type of English-only legislation that threatens to turn the city of Los Gatos into The Cats, or Corpus Christi into Body of Christ. English-only implies that knowing English, and knowing only that one language, is enough. I think the idea that Americans—all Americans—should spend a bit more effort learning at least one other language besides English is a good one, and preferably that other language is one outside the comfort zone of their own heritage. It doesn't even have to be a language that

is spoken outside of America—learning Hawai'ian or Navajo or Cherokee or Inuit will still take us out of English complacency and will help us understand different ways of seeing the world and articulating the experience of life. But I have no patience for these initiatives that tell America: Hey, you should learn *my* language while I ignore *yours*. Spanish complacency among Latinos is just as offensive as the English complacency among Whites of which they complain. Whether we are talking about Mandarin complacency among Chinese-Americans, and so on for every other linguistic group in America, the problem remains the same: it's too much of ourselves and not enough of others.

So, what do we need to make diversity work better, and equally well for ourselves and for others? One thing I would advocate is an English-*first* rule. This is different from English-*only* in that English-first simply means that we all make one language a common priority. This is as essential for social interaction as it is for democracy and diversity. If we don't all have a common language then we cannot all talk to one another, and it seems to me that if there is one thing that Americans should be able to do, anywhere and everywhere in America, it is to talk fluently with one another in a shared language. So if you want to put a Spanish-language introduction on your film, make sure it has English subtitles. If you want to have a sign in Arabic in the front of your Muslim bookstore, make sure it has an English translation. If you want to put a sign in Mandarin in front of your Chinese restaurant announcing daily specials that are not on the menu, make sure it is posted in English as well, so we can all enjoy those specials.

But while English-first implies that we should all make English our common priority, it also implies that something else should come next, and that next thing is our other language. Keep in mind that our other language should not be something that comes from our pre-fab comfort zone, so if you are Latino and you can speak Spanish and English, your work is not yet done. That other language should really be an *other* language, something that drags you out of your comfort zone and forces you to struggle in someone else's tongue and to struggle to see the world as they see it—to strive to understand it completely. As I have said over and over again, diversity is not about promoting ourselves, it is about understanding others.

The work of diversity is hard work, and truly learning another language (and not just a few words of it) is part of that hard work. If you think, "who has time to learn another language? Why, it's ridiculous to expect a Latino to learn Mandarin or some other language!" then I will say this: it is as ridiculous to expect a Latino to learn Mandarin as it is to expect a White person to learn Spanish. If you think it is unrealistic to expect you to learn a truly different language, then stop telling someone else to learn yours. And sure, people might gripe about why English should be the common language and not something else, but I have yet to hear a compelling reason for a language other than English to be the common language for America. And yes, I have heard Latinos say that Spanish was the "original" language of California and so all they are doing is setting things right, but that argument is based on something that in the academic world we refer to as *crap*. Spanish is a colonial language just as much as English, and I do not know at what point sheer delusion set in and Spanish became considered a language of colonized people. If you want to speak an original language of the area that is now California, tell me about it in a truly native language of the region—Nahuatl, Yuki, Hupa, why, I'd even accept Quechua, though it's a bit far afield. But please don't tell me how Spanish is your language of "resistance." I've already said it once and so here I will say it again: *Resistance without reflection is simply the mobilization of idiocy.*

The other language of diversity: political correctness
No other language issue relating to diversity generates more divisive debate and cacophonic controversy than the issue of political correctness. On the surface, it seems an idea with which no one

should take issue: examine the way we speak and the words we use and either take out or find better alternatives for the parts that cause offense to others. Instead of saying "gypsy," for instance, we should use the word "Roma." Simple enough, and it doesn't even take much effort.

So where is the controversy? The controversy emerges over the increasingly aggressive ways that political correctness has been "enforced" by the self-appointed guardians of diversity, to the point where we have gone from the rethinking of our words to reflect empathy toward others to the outright censorship of speech we don't want to hear. The so-called "right not to be offended" by anyone else's words has resulted in a longer and longer list of words and concepts that various groups won't "tolerate," meaning that political correctness has become one of the primary sources of *intolerance* in the framework of diversity. This intolerance, incidentally, is actually presented by its proponents as tolerance, which is why questioning any aspect of political correctness usually results in charges of intolerance, if not outright claims of racism (even if race isn't involved), against those who do the questioning. The growing sense of exasperation that many people have felt, on both the political left and the political right, has been a cause of growing concern because political correctness is starting to look a lot like censorship. And in case you haven't heard, censorship is bad for democracy and it is bad for diversity.

Remember that the reason the Supreme Court has ruled that diversity is an inherent good for society is because diversity allows for the "robust exchange of ideas." Political correctness, which is a part of diversity, has done the opposite: it has prevented and shut down the robust exchange of ideas. Anything that violates the unwritten rules of political correctness is deemed "hate speech," and hate speech must be silenced, or so the argument goes. I agree that hate speech should be called out for what it is, but the problem is that the unwritten rules of political correctness have confused unpopular or alternative ideas with hate speech. Speech you hate to hear is not the same thing as hate speech. The list of "things that cannot be said" grows longer by the day, and many people feel so constrained by the fear of being attacked by the increasingly aggressive enforcement of political correctness by its so-called "radical" proponents that they say nothing at all. Only the silence is robust.

The concern over the ever-expanding reach of political correctness isn't just something that academics discuss and debate on college campuses. It is something that has spilled over into the nation-wide discussion and debate on diversity with its own sort of acrimony and anger. It was certainly a factor in the election campaigns leading up to the November 2016 presidential election. Many supporters of Donald Trump, for instance, actually liked the fact that his comments were often rude and offensive because it exhibited what they felt was a sort of freedom of speech that flew in the face of political correctness. Supporters of Hillary Clinton, of course, denounced Trump as a racist, someone unfit for the presidency due to his penchant for hate speech. If we add the concept of "fake news" to the mix, we get a very distressing outcome in the current moment. While conservatives and the alt-right have taken to dismiss anything they don't want to hear from the political left as fake news, liberals and progressives have taken to dismissing anything they don't want to hear from the political right as hate speech. The space of meaningful political discourse grows smaller and smaller with each passing day.

One example of how this all plays out to very negative ends is the debacle that occurred on UC Berkeley's campus on February 1, 2017, when Milo Yiannopoulos was supposed to speak at UC Berkeley at the invitation of the Berkeley College Republicans but was prevented from doing so by protesters. This isn't the place to analyze who made the mistakes that allowed the situation to devolve into the violence and vandalism that occurred that day on campus (and off). The main thing I want to point out is the way that political correctness was used to prevent Yiannopoulos from speaking at all (ironically his talk was going to focus on how political correctness is used on college campuses to censor conservative viewpoints). Political correctness consists largely of issues relating to diversity, and yet, whether one is on the political left or the political right, the opportunity for the "robust exchange of ideas" that diversity is supposed to bring us, like the space for meaning political discourse, is growing smaller and smaller with each passing day.

Perhaps this is a good moment to quote the ever-insightful Ricky Gervais, who once opined that offense can never be given, only taken. In other words, it's not what is said that should be our concern, but rather our reactions to what is said. The so-called "right not to be offended" relies upon political correctness to identify any and all possible words and phrasings that might offend anyone and then to censor them so that nothing is ever said that could offend anyone. If Ricky Gervais is right, or at least on the right track, perhaps our efforts should be focused on why people seem less and less able to deal with words and ideas that differ from or question their own, or why people let themselves be so offended by an ever-growing list of things. "Hate speech" has a specific, legal meaning—once again, it doesn't refer simply to things we hate to hear.

Walking out of the enclave and into diversity
Collectively, all of these discussions about various aspects of language and diversity bring us back to the problem of the enclave environment. The enclave environment is created by the preference of many identity-based groups to create a localized, non-diverse community—sometimes in the moment (as in the workplace) and sometimes on a permanent basis (as in ethnic-based neighborhoods)—in order to separate themselves from the diversity of society and to opt out of the work that is necessary to make diversity

succeed. There are a number of justifications offered for the creation and persistence of these enclaves—some say they are necessary as a form of protection from the oppression of the dominant group, and others say they are a positive expression of community solidarity—but at the end of the day, they all stand as an impediment to the cultivation of a meaningful and shared sense of diversity that works for all of us.

I have seen enclaves in many places elsewhere in the world where I have worked, just as I have seen them all over America. And wherever I find them, they tend to create problems and they tend to create tension. Under our current standards of what diversity is, and I think I have made clear how inadequate and inappropriate those standards are, we often look at a city and see a bunch of different ethnic neighborhoods and think—wow, so much diversity. But as I have said repeatedly, the passive coexistence of different groups is *not* diversity. This is why the diversity of a city like Los Angeles is such an illusion: it has a diverse array of different identity-based groups, but it does not have diversity. It is a deeply divided city that can better be described as a geographic congregation of different enclaves. I once sat in a meeting in LA's City Hall and listened to city officials talk about each of the many separate parts of Los Angeles, describing each one by its dominant identity group—this place is African-American, that place is Latino, this place is Puerto Rican, that place is Chinese, this place used to be Latino but now it's Korean, and so on. Whatever the reasons for these various enclaves, whether in Los Angeles or anywhere else, the reality is that those barriers have to start coming down if we want diversity to work—*real* diversity that is, complete with meaningful interaction and communication between all of us, whatever identity we think we have or want to have.

I know there are those who will talk about how these enclaves have to exist to provide security and protection for the community and so forth, but let me offer a few personal observations of why I think it is time we put those notions aside and take a sobering look at what we really have in front of us. Before I came to Berkeley, I taught at a university in southern California, and while there I became friends a couple, an American (white) male who had married a woman from China and who had subsequently taken American citizenship. After many years of marriage, one of the things they had decided they would do is to bring her parents, who were living in China, to America to live permanently. Part of the reason for this decision was that the parents were getting older and the couple wanted to be in a position to be able to care for them. Another part of the reason was to bring the parents to America to show them the benefits of living in a democratic society.

The parents eventually came to America, and the couple set them up with all sorts of things, including English language classes, to help them become comfortable in American society and to be able to take advantage of all it has to offer. Yet shortly after the parents arrived, and after they came into contact with the Chinese community in southern California, they quit the English classes and the other things set up for them to adjust to life in America and moved instead to Monterey Park. Monterey Park has a sizeable Chinese population and is known as something of an ethnic enclave. The couple's parents were clear on why they wanted to move: in Monterey Park, they could speak Chinese (Mandarin) at the grocery store, read the signs (which were all in Mandarin), and go to Chinese restaurants and order in Mandarin, and talk with Mandarin-speaking neighbors, and so forth. Learning English was too much work, so why not move to a Chinese enclave where you can still get the benefits of being in America without having to do any of the work of diversity? The Chinese enclave made it possible to be *in* America without actually being *of* America, as strange as that sounds.

Another personal example, and I know this is a common one based on the many conversations I have had with so many other people—and yes, I also know it will be controversial—concerns a Latino couple in northern California who also brought their parents to America. Unlike the couple I knew in southern California, however, the Latino couple's parents came to America illegally, or if you prefer, without documents. You might think it would be hard to function in California (or anywhere in America) speaking only Spanish and no English, but if you move into a Latino enclave, into a neighborhood where everyone speaks Spanish and all of the shops and restaurants have Spanish-speaking staff, it is actually quite easy to do. The parents have been in America at this point for almost 30 years, never seeking American citizenship and never learning English. With both partners in the couple working, when they had children, it was convenient to have their parents act as free daycare for the children, and thus their children grew up in a Spanish-speaking enclave, spending most of their days around their grandparents, who could only speak Spanish. (The grandparents would also earn money under the table by babysitting for other families in the neighborhood, so other children in the neighborhood also grew up in a Spanish-only environment.) As a result, as the children grew, their English skills began to lag far behind what would and quite frankly should be expected of children of the same age entering the American school system. I know there are community-based activists who will argue that this is why we need more funding for bilingual-education programs, but the reality here is that we do not have a failure of the education system—we have a failure of diversity. When Spanish-speakers are flocking to the comfort and homogeneity of Spanish-speaking enclaves, or Chinese (Mandarin)-speakers are flocking to the comfort and homogeneity of Chinese communities, we get the appearance of diversity without any of the substance. And what we really need is the substance.

These two examples are examples of physical enclaves, which take the form of identity-based spaces of self-segregation that relieve people of the work needed for diversity to grow and function properly. There are other forms of enclaves as well. There are *family-community* enclaves, in which people from a particular identity-group may live in different areas but only circulate among those of their extended family or extended community. When I lived in London for a time in the late 1990s, I noticed for instance that members of the Sri Lankan community tended only to interact with one another through extended-family networks, even though many of them worked in various places around London and had ample opportunity to make non-Sri Lankan, British friends. One day I was talking with one of the Sri Lankans, who told me that in spite of working in a large office environment where he was the only person with origins in South Asia, he didn't have a single friend at the office, even after years of working there. When I asked him why, he stated: "they go to pubs and drink beer and socialize…their ways are not our ways." I can't imagine myself living in Sri Lanka and having no Sri Lankan friends, or even thinking of saying "they eat curry and socialize…those are not my ways." My first and primary goal would be to make those ways part of my ways—that's how diversity works (remember, cultural appropriation is necessary for diversity to work). Yet in the case of this Sri Lankan gentleman and his wife, living in London consisted of a small enclave of other Sri Lankans, living in other parts of London, but only visiting one another to recreate as much of Sri Lanka as possible, while avoiding the "ways" of the place they called home—London.

These enclave mentalities can even be projected globally. I remember having a discussion in my office hours with a Korean-American student who was about to graduate. When I asked her what she wanted to do after graduation, she said she was going to get a degree in public health at an American university and then take her education and skills to South Korea to help build that country's health care system and make it better. When I mentioned that South Korea's health care system was already quite excellent, and that there were many other places in the world where her education and skill set would be much more effectively applied, I tossed out, just as an example, Bangladesh. The Korean-America student was awkwardly silent for a moment, and then said—and I remember these words exactly because they disturbed me—"I have no interest in helping those people."

I can't fathom a world-view in which I would see the world as a burning house, and as I ran inside to save people, would try to save only those of my kind. Is this what diversity is supposed to do for us? Latinos run into the house screaming in Spanish to save other Latinos, Koreans scream in Korean for Koreans—suddenly a Bangladeshi woman cries out in Bengali for help, but unfortunately the Latinos only know Spanish and the Koreans only know Korean and neither ever cared to learn Bengali, and so the woman is left to die. *She's somebody else's problem. Wrong ethnicity, wrong language—sorry.* If that's what diversity offers us now, then that's one house that needs to be left to burn to the ground, after of course everyone inside is saved by the less narcissistic and less self-obsessed among us. As for me, I am always interested in helping *those* people, and the reason is simple. I don't live in an enclave. I don't *want* to live in one. No one should.

Then there are *political* enclaves, which are the specialty of all those who consider themselves leaders and activists for "their" community. Every election season in America, I start hearing references to things like the "Asian vote" or the "Latino vote" or the "Black vote" and so on. The idea is to mobilize by political enclave, so that a person who is "Asian" (or Asian-American), for example, need only ask for his or her pre-determined ethnic voting preferences—handed down by community-based "leaders" and "activists"—and then follow along like ants on a sugar trail. Currently, there are those who argue that this is somehow a form of diversity activism, strengthening the voice of the communities, the political enclaves, by mobilizing them to fight for whatever the community needs (as defined by community leaders). But the reality is this: to vote or to participate in democracy based on the pre-set preferences of one's ethnic or racial or any other enclave-style identity group is to express the epitome of democratic laziness. Democracy is an issue-driven political system and to avoid thinking about these issues and to substitute some pre-fabricated perspective based on the cajoling muse of the enclave is to undermine the whole system. It avoids the true work of diversity as much as it avoids the true work of democracy. And yet there are those whose minds have eroded and evaporated to the point where they think this is the "true work" of the grassroots activist: to get the homogeneous enclave to think and vote homogeneously, because somehow homogeneity leads to stronger diversity and better democracy. Sadly, our politicians even cater to this separatist mentality, courting the "Latino vote" or the "Asian vote" and so on, as if people in an identity-group all think alike, as if all people in an identity-group *should* think alike. Yet this kind of activism ends up giving us a democracy and a diversity that are about as dynamic as a sloth stampede in a mattress showroom. For democracy and diversity to function properly and to prosper, we all need to walk out of our self-walled enclaves and walk towards everyone else. The journey from ourselves towards others is the essence of an inter-cultural democracy.

The comfort of sameness: safe spaces
There is probably no clearer example of how and why diversity fails, of how diversity creates endless enclaves of sameness, than the recent trend to construct "safe spaces." A safe space is a physical place open only to people from a specific identity group where they can feel safe from others and where, in a an environment of sameness, they can find solace in a place where "words can't hurt" and the "right not to be offended" is secured. Yes, you read that right. Safe spaces are spaces where we can be protected from diversity.

Safe spaces have emerged on college campuses in connection with the expansion of political correctness.[6] As more and more words and phrases were marked as offensive and insulting, many people felt that merely existing in the company of others had become unbearable—the threat that an offensive word might be uttered, even if unintentionally, created an emotional fear that left many feeling vulnerable. The word "microaggression" was created to refer to the ways that others continuously offended and hurt people in small, almost imperceptible ways. Rather than one giant stab of racism, microaggressions referred to the idea of emotional death by a million racist paper cuts. Life among others was unbearable, so what was needed was a place where we could retreat to sameness and homogeneity, a place where everyone "got it" and understood each other, a beautiful enclave of insiders and a place where outsiders could not enter. Thus was the safe space born.

If you're not sure what a microaggression is, I can give an example or two. I could easily give lots of examples because university administrations all across the country have been sending memo after memo to faculty to tell them what words and phrases should be avoided in conversations with students and with colleagues. One phrase that that has been targeted, for instance, in the context of a job search committee, is anything that sounds like "I think the most qualified person should get the job." That's a microaggression, because it hints at the possibility that other candidates, some of whom might be from minority groups, might not be as qualified as the others. Instead, we should say something like "I think the most deserving candidate should get the job," because that shows that everyone is equally qualified, but one candidate "deserves" the opportunity more than others, so the issue is about fairness

---

6 Conor Friedersdorf, "Campus Activists Weaponize 'Safe Space'," *The Atlantic* (November 10, 2015) at https://www.theatlantic.com/politics/archive/2015/11/how-campus-activists-are-weaponizing-the-safe-space/415080/

rather than qualifications. Another thing a person should never say is something like "Your English is really good," as this is patronizing and either calls out a person's foreignness or implies that they somehow might be less American than someone else (note that even if you know that a person is not American and English is not their first language, you're still not supposed to say this as it is considered inherently hurtful). In spite of the memos, however, some people still keep using these phrases, oppressing others without being aware of it, and thus, safe spaces were created to provide refuge from the tiresome onslaught of oppression that takes place every minute of every day.

Safe spaces come in a variety of formats. Sometimes they can just be a physical space that is set aside only for people from a certain group, an LGBTQI+ lounge, for example. Or they could be something like an Asian-only fraternity or a separate graduation ceremony for black students. As you can probably guess, the one group that cannot have a safe space is the white group, as anything that says "whites only" is considered racist and discriminatory. It might surprise you to hear that I actually agree with the latter point. But I agree with it in the following way: *all* safe spaces are inherently discriminatory. We should no more accept a "whites only" sorority than we should a "blacks only" one.

Safe spaces, which are in essence identity-based enclaves, are ironically presented as sites of diversity. Safe spaces strengthen diversity, the argument goes, because they remind us that we don't yet have enough diversity in American society. Safe spaces will only wither away when we reach a point of full diversity, because only then will oppression and microaggressions come to an end. If you'd like me to translate that into more stark terms, what it means is that safe spaces remind us that there are still too many whites and not enough minorities and persons of color. Since whites are inherently racist and oppressive, and non-whites therefore inherently good and non-oppressive, we have to keep finding ways to add more and more non-whites to visible roles in society, to the point where white oppression is neutralized. Until that happens, safe spaces are provided as shelters from white people.

To my mind, however, and to reiterate again one of the main arguments of this whole project, the reason we have safe spaces is not because we don't yet have enough diversity in American society. *It's because we are doing diversity completely wrong in the first place.* No matter how much more we have of it, at least in its current format, nothing will change. We need to change the way we do diversity first, and only then will safe spaces become unnecessary.

As I have already argued, enclaves are the antithesis of diversity. Since safe spaces are really enclaves, they actively work to undermine the ability of ourselves to relate to and understand others. Safe spaces send the message that safety comes in sameness, which means a safe space inherently rejects diversity merely by its existence. If we are going to have safe spaces, we need to change their purpose. Rather than create them as refuges of homogeneity and sameness, we should instead transform them into spaces that facilitate intercultural communication and interaction. Instead of safe spaces being places where minority groups can gather so that the words of outsiders can't reach them and do their hateful harm, they should instead be places where *anyone* can go and ask questions or say things to others and feel safe from the recriminations of political correctness. That's the only way we can learn about each other. That's the only way the so-called "robust exchange of ideas" can actually happen in the name of diversity. *A safe space should be a hub of intercultural communication and interaction where all are equally welcome.* Anything else will only give us more racism.

There is increasing clamor to expand safe spaces to other environments—grade schools, work places, and so forth. If this happens, it will set the work of diversity back years if not decades. We don't need more spaces of division and exclusivity. We don't need self-inflicted re-segregation in the name of diversity. We don't need more spaces where only some can enter but not others. What we need are spaces where *all* can enter and *all* can participate in the ongoing conversation about ourselves among others.

Tearing down the walls, building up diversity
So what is the work of diversity here? In simple terms, it is to tear down the walls and liberate the enclaves—the physical, the mental, the political, and all the others. It's a scary moment for some, I know, and it requires something of a leap of faith. But all meaningful relationships require a leap of faith—anything from acolyte to zookeeper and everything in between requires a moment where we have to go "all in." Enclaves and safe spaces move in the opposite direction—they are places that allow us to go "all out." Enclaves encourage us to circulate only among ourselves, people who "look like me," in an endless loop of conversation about our community, our home, our problems, our sufferings, our heroes, and so forth. We lose sight of the fact that those are things we should be building in common with each other, not celebrating separately in enclaves. The self-directed, narcissistic nature of enclaves makes the work of diversity so much more difficult, if not altogether impossible.

Enclaves and safe spaces are also predicated on an unbelievably faulty premise. The idea that a place of sameness will provide peace and refuge, a place where there are no hurtful words, no offense is taken or given, and everyone understands each other, borders on the absurd. Japan, South Korea, Bangladesh, and the Maldives, for instance, are all countries that have extraordinarily homogenous populations. Yet all of them also have a long list of divisive problems, and people get offended and hurt every day. Homogeneity provides neither peace nor security. Enclaves and safe spaces are illusions of diversity, and not diversity itself.

Diversity should tear down the walls that separate us, not make them stronger. We need to take the leap of faith, cross the street, walk through the door, take the long way home, take the wrong way home, listen to the different song, speak the different language—whatever it takes. The moment you leave the familiar behind and shed the cloak of repetition and conformity, only then does diversity begin to work its wonderful magic.

※※

Making fun of diversity: an interlude

Something funny about diversity
Another part of the work of diversity—a surprisingly powerful part, I might add—is to laugh. Sure, we all laugh at things pretty much every day, and the ability to laugh is deeply ingrained in the way human beings socialize with one another. But not all laughter is the same—there is silly laughter, cynical laughter, nervous laughter, hysterical laughter, joyful laughter, and so on. Then there is our sense of humor, which can differ from person to person and place to place. Most people, for instance, put considerable importance on a shared sense of humor in judging their compatibility with a potential partner in a relationship. And as for different senses of humor in different cultures, I once found myself in Burma trying to explain why zombie films were funny and entertaining in America, and why *Shaun of the Dead* was a most excellent film. It was pretty much an impossible task: "You see, they're already dead but they need to eat the brains of the living to stay alive, though they are not alive, and the only way to kill the undead is to pretty much blow *their* brains out…oh, man, that's just so funny." My Burmese friends simply stared in consternation. For them, as Buddhists, the proper response would be to show compassion for the zombies. They didn't see the humor at all.

In any case, there is a serious point here—seriously funny, as it were—which is that the ability to laugh at ourselves and at others, both in equal measure and in just the right way, turns out to be an extraordinarily difficult thing to do. And yet at the same time, it is an exceptionally powerful thing to do. It takes work to learn to laugh, to learn to be comfortable enough to laugh, in a way that makes diversity part of the joke, and makes the joke part of diversity. If you ask any stand-up comedian about her or his craft, they will no doubt tell you two things right off the bat: one, comedy is very hard work, and two, laughter is the most powerful thing in the world. The pen might be mightier than the sword, but the well-crafted joke is mightier than both. Comedian Lewis Black once said in one of his routines that the problem with the "enemy"—and here he was referring to radical Muslims who kill in the name of religion, but his point could just as easily refer to any person or any group that takes their identity to be the center of the universe—is that somewhere along the way they lost the ability to laugh. Once you lose the ability to laugh, inhumanity slowly creeps in and corrodes the soul.

At this point, you might be wondering: if laughter is such a good and powerful and natural thing, then why does it require so much work, and how is it part of the work of diversity? Following on a point I made previously, much of the problem we have in the present, and the problem to which we need to devote our work, is that we have what might be called *enclaves of laughter*. Enclaves of any sort, I have argued, are not good, so obviously enclaves of laughter are not good either—certainly nothing to laugh at, and more appositely something to lament and something to resist. Enclaves of laughter occur because in our current state of diversity we have created identity-based boundaries that limit and censor what we can say and do, and when it comes to comedy, the problem is that we believe only certain comics can make certain kinds of jokes, and only certain kinds of people can laugh at them. Once those types of boundaries are created, laughter either loses its revolutionary force, or else it must *use* that revolutionary force to break down those boundaries. For my part, I advocate the latter: when it comes to diversity, a laugh riot would always be better than a street riot.

Comics, along with jesters, jokesters, and pranksters, have always been associated with the margins of society. They tend to be people who tease or test the limits of what is considered proper and normal and decent in any social or cultural context, and so by default they are considered insurrectionary. I once gave a commencement address entitled "The Politics of Laughter" and part of that speech consisted of naming a depressingly long list of comedians around the world who are currently languishing away as political prisoners in various countries or who have simply been assassinated. After I gave this commencement address, a member of the press who covered the talk shared with me his favorite comic cartoon. It is a picture of a clown, standing before an executioner and about to kneel down at the chopping block to be beheaded, and so the clown simply asks, "Why?" The executioner responds: "Because you made us think."

Identity has always been a central theme in comedy, and that is one of the many reasons it plays such a central role in re-framing the way we look at diversity. On the one hand, we have now, just as we have always had, the phenomenon of ethnic jokes. Ethnic jokes play on and at the same time question the various stereotypes and caricatures we have of different cultures—ethnic jokes are always about *other* ethnic groups—but the not-so-well-kept secret about ethnic jokes is that every culture has them. I've never been anywhere in the world, or in any cultural environment, where ethnic jokes of one sort or other did not exist. There was a time in America when Polish jokes were all the rage, but these days you rarely hear them (I'm not lamenting that). And if you think it is because diversity has created a new sensitivity towards cultural difference, then you'd be mighty naïve and grotesquely misinformed. No, our current approach to diversity has simply driven them underground or transformed the way they are told. One interesting recent trend I have noticed is that racist jokes are on the rise, but they are told as private racist jokes with a sort of ironic wink, as if to say: this is funny and racist, but my racism is wrapped in irony so it's cool. More importantly to note is that the tellers of these privately-told racist jokes are quite often from ethnic minority groups. I've even had students come to my office hours and tell me racist jokes, jokes they would never say in public, but only in private—and no, these aren't white students engaging in dominant racism, these are students from all different identity groups. Like little comic speakeasies where we can imbibe a taste of forbidden humor, the hush-hush din of racist jokes still persists as a sort of background hum of resistance to the stifling effects of political correctness.

The hysterical insurgency of diversity
So, if on the one hand we have ethnic jokes to test the limits of identity and humor, what is on the other hand? On the other hand, we have comedians who *do* perform in public, unlike the private circulation of ethnic and racist jokes, but who use their comedic platform to test or to bend and sometimes to challenge or even smash our existing conceptions of identity. One early pioneer of this was the late and great Lenny Bruce. Lenny Bruce would often start his comedic gigs by driving head-on into every word and concept about identity that made people uncomfortable, and the idea was to use the power of comedy to bring that discomfort right into the performance and then skillfully deprive it of its discomfiting effect by transforming it from serious to satirical. Nothing was off limits for Lenny Bruce: Irish people, black people, Jewish people, gay people—all of the stuff that society wanted to sweep under the rug, Lenny Bruce swept it back out and brought it into the open and used laughter as an instrument of liberation. One of his most classic bits, made into a short, animated film, is a bit about the Lone Ranger, who goes by the name "The Masked Man." In the

short film, The Masked Man comes to town as your standard white hero on horseback who saves the people of the village from harm, and then when they offer him anything he wants, he first asks for an Indian (a stand-in for Tonto), with whom he wants to engage in an "unnatural act," and then asks for a horse, with whom he also wants to engage in an "unnatural act." Suddenly, the puritanical image of the Lone Ranger, the epitome of the good white male hero, is broken down into a person who has an interest in both interracial homosexuality *and* zoophilia, leaving the people of the town disgusted. Not everyone found Lenny Bruce's rebellious humor acceptable, and several times he came up against censorship and the long arm of the law. In 2003, Lenny Bruce was actually granted a posthumous pardon for an obscenity conviction he received when George Pataki was governor of New York. Apparently, it was only in hindsight that the force of his comic genius became officially acceptable.

Perhaps even more than Lenny Bruce, I would single out Richard Pryor in the category of absolute genius when it comes to the use of humor to make us think and talk about all those elements of identity that we are normally too afraid to talk about. Richard Pryor was one of the very few comedians who could have an audience rolling on the floor in laughter, and then stop almost mid-sentence and talk seriously about something—racism, for instance—and then head back to comedy, and do it in a way that was as flawless as it was seamless. Provocative, controversial, eloquent, and of course funny, Richard Pryor paved a trail that made possible almost all of what passes for comedy in the present.

Think, for instance, of all of the contemporary comedians who are fighting to continue what Richard Pryor and Lenny Bruce started. Dave Chappelle developed a hilarious skit for his short-lived comedy series *Chappelle's Show*, in which he enlisted the help of musician John Mayer to "test" if different racial groups could be stereotyped by musical genres. When rock n' roll was played, seemingly normal white people—office workers, professionals, and so forth—suddenly got angry and rebellious and wanted to fight, while blacks and Latinos remained indifferent and had no reaction. Next they travel to a barbershop, and when a drummer starts to play, all of the blacks in the barber shop spontaneously start rapping, while the Hispanics simply carry on with their business. But then an electric piano is introduced, and immediately the Hispanics start dancing, while the blacks get back to their work. Finally, when rock n' roll is played in the barber shop, the blacks and Hispanics immediately stop and one black haircutter tells John Mayer to stop playing and "shut the f__k up!" In its entirety, the skit brilliantly addresses and skewers our perceptions about ourselves and others, as much of Dave Chappelle's comedy does.

No doubt, many would be and were offended by these skits and others, but the goal here is to use comedy to break down and move past the fear of causing offense, using comedy so that we begin to talk about the things we are usually afraid to talk about.

If there is one line that represents the ultimate line to cross in comedy, however, it is the line that surrounds the use of the N-word. Lenny Bruce talked about it, Richard Pryor talked about it, and Chris Rock has an absolutely brilliant bit about the only time it is acceptable for a white person to use the N-word. *South Park* has a whole episode about the word, in which the character Randy Marsh mistakenly answers a Wheel of Fortune puzzle (where the answer is supposed to be "naggers") with the N-word. The rest of the episode parodies all of the hypersensitivity that surrounds this one word. Dave Chappelle had a skit on his show in which a white family had the last name Niggar, obviously a homonym for the N-word, and uses the disorientation of hearing that word associated with a white family to show both the power and the impotence of the word itself. Even better from Dave Chappelle is his brilliant skit about a black white supremist. The white supremacist is black but is also blind so doesn't know he is black, and all of his white followers are horrified to see his real identity when he finally pulls off the white pointy hood (KKK style) that covers his face.

The equal right of laughter?
What all of these skits and shows do is to raise the question of *how* we can joke about the issues of diversity, *when* we can joke about diversity-related issues, and *who* has the right to joke about them. Not everyone in comedy fares so well in wading into this territory. Former Seinfeld actor Michael Richards went on a rant in one of his shows in 2006 in which he used the N-word several times. He claims he meant no offense and was using it as "shock value," but the public jury was not convinced and declared this particular instance to be racist rather than funny. So how do we know when humor is constructive and when it is destructive? Should we take the Lenny Bruce approach and just start saying the N-word—at all times and places—so that eventually it becomes so common that it loses its racist power? Or should we go the route of Richard Pryor, who at one point in one of his stand-up performances declared that all of us, including African-Americans, should just stop saying the N-word completely? I'm not going to answer that question right now—not to avoid it but because I will discuss it later in a different context—but what I do want to point out is that the debate over the use of the N-word in comedy is actually related to a larger question in the world of comedy that is perhaps equally difficult to answer. The question is this: who has the right to tell a joke about whom, and once we decide that, for whom is it acceptable to laugh at that joke?

    I will offer an example using a joke that I heard at a reception at UC Berkeley a few years ago. The hosts of the reception had hired a local bay area comic to do a short performance, and at this point I have forgotten the name of the comic, not because he wasn't famous, but because he wasn't funny. One other thing you need to know about this joke is that in India, the one ethnic group that gets continuously made fun of are the Punjabis (named for the region in north-west India called Punjab). Here is the joke as it was told: "Punjabis are the Latinos of the Indian community—they never want to work and they are always looking for an excuse to drink." I should mention also at this point that the comic was of Indian heritage and that about two-thirds of the crowd at the reception were also of Indian heritage or actually from India. Personally, I found the joke both tasteless and useless, yet the crowd—especially the Indian part of it—laughed heartily. Others looked uncomfortable, but then the comic added the magic line that so many so-called "ethnic" comics like to use: "It's okay for me to tell that joke because I'm Indian."

The whole idea of a comic saying it is okay to make a joke because they are in essence "not white" stems from the erroneous belief—one that I have discussed at length already—that only white people can be racist. That belief gives rise to the sense of permissiveness that says a comic of Indian descent can say pretty much anything he wants and somehow, no matter how offensive it seems, it can never be racist (or offensive). If a white person tells the joke, it is racist; if an Indian tells the same joke, it is comedy. One other thing I should point out about this example is that the reception was a South Asian-related event, which is why most of the audience consisted of persons from South Asia or of South Asian heritage. Not a single Latino person was present to hear the joke, and if you are wondering why that is, it's because of another trend I have discussed earlier, namely the narcissism of diversity. The Latinos will most likely be found at the Latin American Studies reception, which is where you won't find South Asians.

So I wonder if the claim of the comic holds true. If I took this rather uncomical comic into a venue where the audience was mostly Latino, would it really be okay to tell that joke? My guess is that it would not only fail to amuse but it would also most likely offend, and I don't think the "hey, I'm not white" card would buy immunity. Daniel Tosh had a bit in his program *Tosh.0* called "Is it racist?" and I think if I were able to post a recording of that joke, just as it was told, then people would have no problem calling it racist.

I have raised this issue of where and how lines of identity get drawn in comedy in my lectures and in my classes. Some people make the claim that as long as a comic is making fun of every group and not just some groups (or one group), then it's okay. The idea is that if you make fun of everyone, then it's probably okay. Others feel strongly that only comics from the identity group that is the subject of the joke can make that joke—blacks can make fun of blacks, whites can make fun of whites, Latinos can make fun of Latinos, and so on, but those lines cannot be crossed. I even brought up the joke I used in the example above in one of my lectures, and one member of the audience who identified himself as an American of Indian heritage said that the joke is funny but only if told by someone who is Indian or of Indian heritage. Otherwise it would be racist. When I asked if it would be acceptable if a Latino told the same joke but in reverse (as in, Latinos are the Punjabis of the Hispanic community), he replied that in that case it would definitely be offensive. In this case, we end up with *enclaves of laughter*, where only certain comics with certain identities can tell certain jokes, and only certain people with certain identities can laugh at them. And if that is what diversity ends up giving us in the present, then what we need is a new kind of diversity, and a new kind of humor to deliver it.

I will admit that I am disheartened at times by the trend in recent years for comics to use their ethnic or racial or religious (or any other identity-category) as the default calling card for their jokes. It seems to me as lazy an approach to crafting comedy as the retort of "so's your mom" to, well, anything. I understand that all comics draw on personal experience for their material, but it might be time to go back to the well-spring of subversion that is the font of the comedian's lexicon and use it to push diversity into new and unexpected but very necessary directions. I do tire quickly of the amateurish moments when comedians try to cross identity lines and you get a black comedian unloading jokes about how "white people can't dance" or Latino comedians barking out how "Asians are good at math" and so forth. I also tire of enclave humor, where for instance black comics tell jokes aimed only at a black audience and everyone else has to laugh nervously and politely to show that they can "tolerate diversity." Comedy is probably the best place to chart a new path to crossing identity lines, both on the stage and in the audience, because that's what comedy has always done—cross lines. Comedians have to craft new material to take us there, and we as an audience have to be brave enough to listen and bold enough to laugh.

I've already mentioned the point made by Ricky Gervais that offense is taken, never given. Gervais is certainly a comedian who knows a thing or two about crossing lines and even about taking those lines and tying them in knots just to show you he can and just to watch what you do in response. (On that note, do look up the episode of *The Office* where he tries to tell a joke about a black man's penis at an office party.) One of the things that makes comedic dialog so different from every other sort of communication is that comedy asks us, and indeed, requires us to suspend our sense of what is expected and appropriate and then make ourselves susceptible to something unexpectedly different. Diversity cannot be transformed entirely through comedy, but comedy can do things in ways that sometimes nothing else can. It's an insurrection in words, a revolution of laughter. And it doesn't have to come from a stage either. It ought to flow through our dialog, the way we talk and speak and interact when we are out in public and even when we are in private—any time we are ourselves among others. Sometimes it is even when we are just among ourselves. Learning to laugh at others and among others is only part of what makes comedy work: it's the ability to laugh *at* ourselves and *by* ourselves that has the potential to set us truly free. Without that, the work of diversity will never be done.

End of comedic interlude

Doing the work of diversity
The work of diversity has all too often been the work that we expect someone else to do. Those who fight for more affirmative action, for instance, usually on the mistaken ground that affirmative action creates more diversity, are in essence advocating that the government take up the work of diversity, that policymakers do something about it. Similarly, just because the Supreme Court has finally made a decision on same-sex marriage, this doesn't mean that somehow diversity has occurred. It means only that one government institution has allowed same-sex couples to join in the normative legal relations of matrimony the rest of society has enjoyed for so long (not everyone would use the word "enjoy" when it comes to marriage). But if we look at diversity not as the passive coexistence of different groups, which is the dominant platform of diversity that we currently have, and instead look at diversity as the active process of understanding others, then there is nothing that a court decision or a piece of legislation can do that would substitute for the work that *we ourselves* need to do to transform diversity into something that truly works equally for all of us.

To review the points I have made, here in summarized form are some of the most important things that we can and indeed *must* do to transform diversity into an active and equally inclusive process. What they all have in common, and what separates them from our current passive models of diversity, is that they all require us to cultivate a sense of fortitude and integrity, and to do so on our own.

The list

(1) *To liberate ourselves from the idea of "going back."* It is difficult if not impossible to build a collective sense of trust if you continuously have one foot out the door, or one eye on an open window.
(2) *To liberate ourselves from the enclave, in whatever form that enclave occurs.* It is nothing but sheer hypocrisy to demand more diversity from society if you do so from the safety of a non-diverse, homogeneous enclave.
(3) *To liberate ourselves from the seductive sound of our own voices in our own tongues.* If diversity comes in a number of different sounds, the only thing that separates noise from music is learning to understand all the different sounds. The language of diversity is the new language you learn, not the language you already know.
(4) *To liberate ourselves from the fear of laughter, and to use laughter to liberate ourselves from our fears.* This is not the time for nervous laughter, polite laughter, cynical laughter, bitter laughter, or derisory laughter. The revolution is here, and it's hysterical.
(5) *To liberate ourselves from the self-centric view of diversity and move toward a new way of situating ourselves among others.* To paraphrase a point I made earlier: diversity is about learning to walk in someone's else shoes, and not about praising the beauty and comfort of our own.

Diversity and its true grit
The grit of the matter is this: diversity is hard work and it is endless work. Yo-Yo Ma may be a master of the cello, but if you ask him,

I am quite sure he will not be able to tell you on which day or in which year he finished mastering it. Even someone of his musical caliber still has to practice every day, and can still find new sounds and new techniques to learn. Too many people have been lulled to an intellectual sleep by the lullaby of the easy and simplistic fix—just a little more affirmative action, just a little more immigration reform, and finally we get diversity, finally we've mastered the challenge. And when it doesn't work, we hear the usual incessant complaint: there's still too much racism, oppression, colonialism, imperialism, etc. Affirmative action won't fix things, immigration reform won't fix things, fighting for the rights of "your people" in your enclave community won't fix things. We've already tried those things, we've already heard that tiresome song far too many times. This sort of complacent and formulaic sloganeering can only be considered a form of activism by the dead and the foolish—it's enough to make Pete Seeger break his banjo over a bald eagle's head in a fit of nonviolent rage. *We shall overcome?* We shall overcome nothing if we cannot overcome ourselves.

Diversity is a collective responsibility—it is not something that one group provides for another, it is not something that one group is responsible for more than another, and it is not a social service the government provides for us. We've tried that and it doesn't work, and it doesn't work because it *can't* work. It's up to us to reach across the divides between us, and it's up to us to learn the languages that make it possible to talk across those divides and to put diversity in our own collective words. It's up to us to make the necessary choices and to do the necessary work. Sure, there are certain things the government can do—there are lots of different pieces to the diversity puzzle, and citizen-based action is only effective in a democratic context when citizens at some point interact with the officials that are supposed to represent them. But there has been far too much reliance on what officials need to do, and not enough on what *we* need to do, and since we are both the components and constituents of diversity, it seems to me we all need to be more involved. I'm not talking about joining your local chamber of commerce or singing in the community college choir, though both of those are fine things to do. The moment you step out of your house, or the moment you choose what music to listen to or what show to watch—so many moments that make up opportunities to choose—you in essence vote for the kind of diversity you want.

I understand the fear that everyone has, and I understand the trepidation that is created by the call to action for crafting a new diversity for America. No one wants to be the first person to walk out of the enclave, because there is a considerable amount of credibility—"street cred" for lack of a more formal phrase—that is built up just by existing in the homogeneous environment of one's "community." To walk away from that, or to consider a new set of values, no matter how much better they might make things in the long run, is to risk losing that credibility and losing one's community. Those mired in the comfort of community, those weighed down by the heavy anchor of narcissistic complacency, will call you a sell-out or will call you uppity or out you as an outsider or any one of a number of names meant to shame you, when in fact the shame is on them. But there is something very strange here, especially when all of this is done in the name of social justice and community building and so forth.

Have you ever had one of those moments when you look back in history and ask yourself: how could a slave-owner not know what he was doing was wrong? How could a plantation owner not look out from his porch, of her porch for that matter, and not think, wow, this is nothing but sheer inhumanity—time to set these slaves free and do this work on my own? How could an auctioneer at a slave auction not have a moment where he just condemned the whole thing in front of his peers and then walked away? The answer to those questions, I'm afraid, is easier to fathom than any of us care to think.

You see, the reason that the plantation owner didn't free his slaves and then do the work himself, or at least do it alongside his newly-freed slaves to whom he was now paying a fair wage, is because the *social* cost of doing so was prohibitively high. Aside from the ridicule from all of his former peers and friends, who would no doubt call him the nineteenth-century equivalent of a sell-out, if the plantation owner dared to ask of his other plantation-owner colleagues that they too follow suit and treat all other human beings with equal respect, he would face immediate ostracism. No more invitations to the club, no more banter over mint juleps on the neighbor's porch, no more idle afternoons during the heat of the day in which to play a leisurely game of cards while others toiled miserably in the fields under the miserable midday sun. And you might think—well, those things don't really sound all that important to me. But if you are a plantation owner in the south, it's everything you know and it's everything you value. All of your social status and social respect, all of your future opportunities and potential, all of your potential brides (or husbands), all of the comfort of the only life you have known—all of it is dependent upon maintaining things the way they are. It's plantation cred, so to speak. For those who would want change, the price is catastrophic, and the social pressure for conformity is intense. In a strangely unexpected way—and here I will drag this example back to the present—the forces and attractions that keep the slave-owner immersed in racism are the same as those that keep the hip-hop star immersed in rap culture or the trust-fund kid immersed in privilege or the cowboy immersed in the rodeo or the southern Baptist immersed in church. It doesn't necessarily mean that any of those identities are fake. It just means that identities sometimes run deep and changing them takes a lot of work. The work of diversity is hard work precisely for that reason, but it's good work, too.

And so how do we best do the work of diversity? In our current abysmal state of diversity, the hip-hop star and the trust-fund kid and the cowboy and the southern Baptist all exist in their own separate worlds, and for some reason we call the existence of these separate and parallel worlds diversity. But how can we call the passive existence of these and so many other worlds diversity? There is no understanding between them, no conversation across the divides, just separate worlds with separate languages and separate sets of values. But me, I am naive to the point of revolution, and I think that we will only get a true sense of diversity, one that is meaningful and constructive and equally accessible to all, when the trust-fund kid walks into the southern Baptist church, and when the southern Baptist walks into the hip-hop concert, when the hip-hop star walks into country, and when the cowboy walks into the trust-fund world. And again, it's not about walking the walk and talking the talk—it's about understanding. The best way to question and test our sense of ourselves is to try to understand the sense of others, and for them to do the same in return. I understand the fear that goes along with those first steps outside of the enclave, the moment of vulnerability, the moment when you realize there is no going back. But after the moment of vulnerability passes, we get something new and we get something that finally looks like diversity. We don't have to travel to Mars to look for new forms of life. We can find them and create them right here on Earth, right in our own backyard, right at the shop on the corner, right in every move we make. Things can be different, things can be better—I know this because I've seen glimpses. Take the chance and walk with me. I'll even give you my shoes.

CHAPTER 2

COURTING DIVERSITY

I once had the opportunity to spend a summer in Helsinki, Finland. It was a research trip, centered around the question of why Finland seemed to have so little corruption. One day early in the summer I ended up in a supermarket in central Helsinki, hoping to stock up on a few things for my otherwise empty apartment. While I was perusing the various items that stared back at me from the shelves of the aisle, I saw something that caught my eye and made me do a double-take. I looked directly at this product, and it took my mind a few seconds to process the information while I stared at the label in a trance of incredulousness. But no, my eyes did not deceive me, and the horror of that moment still lives with me today. There, in the middle of a shelf on the sauce aisle, stood a jar of something that looked a bit like regurgitated baby food, with an unappetizing reddish-brown color, and labeled quite prominently in English: "American Sauce."

The only thing that allowed me to quell the tsunami of nausea that was welling up inside me was the amusing realization that had I lost my lunch on the floor of the supermarket, any employee coming to clean it up wouldn't know if I was sick or if I had simply dropped a jar of American Sauce on the floor. As I fought through the waves of horror and nausea—they were coming fast and strong, as if the contents of my stomach were in labor—I decided to have a look at the ingredients, perhaps searching for a clue as to what sorts of things this Frankensauce was made from. I couldn't quite sort out everything that had gone into this mess of a food source, but my best guess was that it was some weird blend of ketchup, mustard, mayonnaise, perhaps some pickle relish, and maybe a few artificial bacon bits—not really sure. My hands were shaking as I read the label, and my eyes were blurry from the perspiration that slowly dripped down my forehead. But the strangest moment of realization I had was that somewhere in Finland, maybe in Helsinki or some other town, maybe after that wonderful Finnish ritual known as the sauna, somewhere in Finland a Finnish family was sitting down to dinner with a jar of that cultural abomination on the table and thinking: "Oh boy! It looks like we're having American food tonight!"

Don't get me wrong—Finland is a wonderful place with wonderful people. But that sauce—ugh—that sauce would never in a million years pass any test for what "American food" is or might be. It would be like eating an enchilada with chopsticks and calling it Chinese food. It's unnatural. It's disturbing. But there it was. But it does raise the question of how we might actually test to see if something qualifies as American food—beyond something patently obvious like a deep-fried Snickers bar. And the question of how we could test something to see if it is genuinely American food raises the question—and here comes my segue...wait for it, wait for it—of how we could test something to see if it is the right thing to do for diversity. I mean, I've already talked about the hard work of diversity. But when we have a moment where we have the opportunity to do something for diversity, no matter how big or small it is, how do we know what the right thing to do is? How do we know what will work best for diversity? How do we know what will take us in the right direction, or at least move us out of all the nonsense we have now that we *think* passes for diversity?

I am going to offer a way to answer each of these questions one step at a time, in the form of a how-to guide to determine the right direction to go, a sort of DDIY (as in, definitely-do-it-yourself) manual for anyone interested in giving it a try. And I do hope if you are reading this, you are also hoping to give it a try. The first step in the right direction is to figure out why this seemingly simple transformation of diversity into being about *others* more than *ourselves* is such a frustratingly difficult action to start. The short answer is that we have developed an odd habit that is extraordinarily difficult to break, and that is the habit of seeking out sameness and avoiding difference. We broadcast who we are (or who we think we are), and wait for the signals from others that match with ours, and then gravitate towards them. We call this diversity, but we treat it like we are in a perpetual search for a soul mate, someone with absolute compatibility. But with diversity, we're not looking for compatibility—we're looking for *incompatibility*, and more than that, we are searching for ways to understand incompatibility and change it into compatibility. We think we are square pegs who can't wait to jump into the cozy comfort of our square holes, when in fact we should be square pegs looking for round holes, or triangle holes, or rhombus holes, and so on. We should be courting diversity, seeking out difference and trying to come to terms with it. *That's* the work of diversity. First I am going to show how our bad habit works in practice, and then I am going to offer a somber exercise of how it plays out with divisive consequences by looking at the Trayvon Martin trial and its aftermath. And with that little road map preview in place, let's jump to the first order of business, something I call *posturing*.

How to correct one's posture
For starters, a definition: *posturing is the public display of identity in such a way as to elicit approval from or express attraction to the collective values of a particular group*. Posturing is thus a way of affirming group-think by creating a public expression of group-based identification. It

tends to be a reflex action, and that is part of the problem. It already takes us one step further from the sort of deep and introspective thought we ought to be doing about our identities and about the way we behave when we walk with and among others. In a very simple way, for instance, consider the example of tagged introductions to various news stories or events of the day. A straightforward question, for instance, would sound something like this: "Did you hear about what happened yesterday in Botswana?" Now let me rephrase the question into a tagged question with a bit of ideological posturing: "Did you hear the story on NPR about what happened in Botswana yesterday?" Now the person asking the question is looking for affirmation of like-mindedness. Listening to NPR—National Public Radio—is something that those of a liberal political viewpoint like to do, so in asking the question this way, the question is really asking me two things: Did I hear about what happened in Botswana yesterday, and am I a fellow liberal? It's a form of posturing because it is asking me to identify myself in some general way to see if there are grounds for affinity. Being the trollmeister that I am, I sometimes like to respond to questions like these by saying something like, "No, I spent the whole day watching Fox news," which, whether true or not, in a place like Berkeley is usually followed by having the original questioner grunt incomprehensibly in disbelief while gasping for air, followed by the traditional throwing of feces in a simian act of aggressive disapproval.

I should also state up front that I am aware of the phrase "virtue signaling" that has become all the rage in recent years, and while my definition of posturing might sound similar to virtue signaling, there is a crucial difference.[7] Virtue signaling has become

---

7 If you're unfamiliar with virtue signaling, see James Bartholomew, "I invented 'virtue signalling'. Now it's taking over the world," *The Spectator* (October 10, 2015) at https://www.spectator.co.uk/2015/10/i-invented-virtue-signalling-now-its-taking-over-the-world/

almost universally used to attack what is seen as liberal hypocrisy, and refers to the act of displaying moral superiority without actually doing anything moral or superior. Putting up a "Black Lives Matter" sign on one's lawn or in a front window without actually doing anything to help improve black lives is an example of virtue signaling (often associated with "slacktivism"). *Posturing*, as I am presenting it, has no ideological bias, and applies equally to both conservatives and liberals. My focus here is also less on the display of moral superiority and more on the method of seeking out sameness, those who are "just like me."

I was once giving a lecture on how to be an informed consumer of the news, and was talking about how to spot bias—from the political left *and* the political right—in various news sources. There is nothing inherently wrong with bias, in the news or anywhere, as long as we, as consumers of information, know how to spot it and know how to account for it in the process of making up our own minds. But in this particular case, I remember a comment from someone in the audience who took issue with my presentation by asking how anyone could watch Fox News because, as she put it, it was just *so* biased. When I pointed out that everyone knows that Fox News approaches things from a conservative viewpoint—that's not really a secret and Fox News is not trying to hide it anyway—and then added that shows like NPR also have their own bias, she blurted out, "Yeah, *biased towards the truth!*" I was giving this talk in San Francisco, so the comment was immediately followed by all sorts of whelps of approval, some applause, and the kind of owl-like head movements people often make in situations like this to see if they can find someone who isn't expressing their approval strongly enough—that is, who isn't *posturing*—so that they can unleash their stares of derision and animosity until that person fully assimilates to the majority opinion of the audience. What I hate about those moments is that they effectively shut down any chance of intelligent discussion or mutual understanding. What seems like intelligence on the surface is actually a form of collective ignorance.

As for me, I listen to and read the news from a wide variety of ideological sources. I especially like to read news about America in foreign newspapers. And no, I am not ideologically confused. Nor do I feel like I am "listening to the enemy" when I listen to one or the other. Posturing tells me I have to choose sides, as if my brain was a cerebral football game and I had to root for only one team, as if I needed to face-paint parts of my cerebrum so that everyone knows whose side I am on. Once I pick a side, I had better not change, and what is more, wherever I go I have to sit with people from my own team so we can collectively commend ourselves on how right we always are. That would be great for me because at some point I can just stop thinking and go into mental cruise control. But in fact I don't do that because I find it ethically and morally indefensible. I listen to and read the news from every political viewpoint—liberal and conservative, domestic and foreign—because I want to understand the different points of view on their own terms. I don't have to be a conservative to understand a conservative point of view, and I don't have to be a liberal to understand a liberal point of view. What I do want to do however is to develop a morally and ethically justifiable way to reach what I think is the best course of action on any particular issue. In other words, I want to think for myself, using all the information I have available to me from a variety of different points of view to reach the best conclusion I can.

Is it more work to do so? Of course it is. But if I haven't made it clear by now, anything worth fighting for is hard work, and so if you are expecting a revolution to happen in the world of diversity by thinking The One and Same Thought over and over again, then you'd better stock up on Twinkies and Mountain Dew (granola and organic artisanal Root Beer if you are in Berkeley) because it's gonna be a long time comin' before that revolution ever happens.

Posturing, you see, is the inverse of diversity: whereas diversity requires us to seek out and understand points of view and ways of life that are different from our own, posturing is a social antic, a narcissistic one-person street theater, if you will, that broadcasts a code designed to identify all like-minded people. It helps us avoid understanding things that are different by helping us locate what is already the same, what is already "like us" and what already "looks like me." It is a form of thought-avoidance that helps us find islands of homogeneity where we can take shelter from the scary world of individual responsibility and cerebral activity. In a way, it's sort of like a physical version of Facebook.

So, what's a person to do? The best way to put an end to the practice of posturing is to start a new practice, and along the lines of what I have been saying throughout this book, one of the most powerful things one can do to create change here is *unembed the self from the enclave,* to walk away from the posturing group to find a free space in which to evaluate whatever matter is at hand. Only the liberation of the self from the group—removing the training wheels, as I have phrased it—creates an open space for self-reflective and evaluative thought, and an open space to reach across to other points of view to understand different perspectives. Only that kind of self-made revolution creates the open society that is required of both democracy and diversity.

Is this sort of advocacy of the revolution of the self really just a form of Western individualism in disguise? No—not at all. I do hear things like that from time to time, but those kinds of criticisms make about as much sense as saying that only Arabs can be good Muslims. Sure, Islam had its start in Arab culture, but anyone can be a good Muslim, and any Arab can be a bad Muslim. There are prisoners of conscience sadly filling jail cells all around the world for the crime of using their own brain and not following the temptation to posture, and yes, the dictators who run the regimes that throw them into jail love to claim that those prisoners are bad because they have been "tainted" by Western thoughts. But no prisoner of conscience is languishing in a cell and thinking: Why and when did I become Western? So no, posturing is not a form of Westernization, nor is it a form of individualism cloaked as something else. It is simply a plea to take the first step towards an active understanding of all that is different and all that is challenging in the world. That's what the essence of diversity is.

Posturing in Play: The Trayvon Martin case
On July 14, 2013, after months of build-up and after weeks of courtroom drama, the verdict in the case of the shooting death of Trayvon Martin was announced: George Zimmerman was acquitted of all charges and was in essence allowed to walk free. I don't really need to go into all the details of the incident that led up to the trial—the tragic confrontation between security guard George Zimmerman and Trayvon Martin which left Martin dead and Zimmerman claiming self-defense under Florida's "Stand Your Ground" law—because those details are widely available elsewhere. Instead I am more interested in exploring how this case came to be a case about identity, and to look for ways that posturing undermines the search for social justice and diversity and equality in America.

The case was widely seen as yet another "test case" for diversity, to see if civil rights and race-relations had improved since, say, the Rodney King trial and the riots that followed that verdict in Los Angeles in 1992. Trayvon Martin was a young, African-American male, unarmed at the time of the shooting, which occurred while he was walking home from a local convenience store, while George Zimmerman was an older "white Hispanic" (more on which in a moment) with a gun and a somewhat vague mandate to provide neighborhood security. Once the identity aspects of the two persons involved in this deadly confrontation became known, however, it became as much an issue of identity as an issue of justice. The two issues became entangled in ways that confused and distorted both. The problem with viewing these types of cases as battles of identity is that they end up becoming predetermined verdicts: if the perpetrator is from a dominant identity group, and if the victim of the crime was from a non-dominant identity group, then promoting "civil rights" means that the verdict *has* to be guilty. In this case, Trayvon Martin was African-American and was also the victim of the crime, and by the simplistic calculus of racial justice, there could only be two outcomes: guilty, which means diversity and justice, or not guilty, which means racism and injustice.

How did we get to such a simplistic way of viewing the legal system, and mixing it up with other issues of identity in ways that may or may not make any sense? Part of this can be explained by posturing. From the start of the trial, based solely on the identity of the victim, so-called community leaders and other self-appointed experts made it clear: if you believed in "racial justice," or if you were from a non-dominant (minority) group, then you had only one possible choice to make—*guilty*. You end up having to affirm group identity by taking the "right" public posture on this issue. Battle lines get drawn by identity, rather than by knowledge of the law or knowledge of the specific case. You have to stand on one side or the other. You're either with us or against us. It's as simple as that. It's also a complete disaster for both justice and diversity.

One of the first clues that this was a case where identity was on trial more than justice was the confused manner in which the very identity of George Zimmerman was presented. Though George Zimmerman identified as Hispanic, right from the start of the reporting about the incident he was described instead as "white Hispanic," a nearly nonsensical and seemingly contradictory description of a person's identity. He was referred to as white Hispanic because his mother was Latino and his father was white. And if you think, well, then it makes sense to call him white Hispanic, then ask yourself this question about someone else you may know:

when was the last time you heard President Obama referred to as a "white black" president? My guess is never, so why then do we end up with a "white Hispanic" George Zimmerman? The most important reason is that posturing would be much more difficult if not impossible without this strange categorization. Since the battle lines of racial justice are always drawn—quite erroneously in my opinion—as dominant (white) group versus non-dominant (non-white) minorities, to have a victim from one non-dominant group (African-America) and a perpetrator from another non-dominant group (Hispanic) would complicate the racial posturing that simplifies racial justice into a majority-minority issue. It also creates, if we accept the argument that the killing was racially justified, the awkward moment when the thing-that-cannot-be-mentioned—namely minority-on-minority racism—rears its ugly but ever-present head. By adding an element of "whiteness" to George Zimmerman, it becomes easier to make the tragic confrontation between the two men and the trial that followed into a struggle for racial justice, pitting the victimized minority against a privileged majority.

I would also like to point out another aspect of identity that was not championed or scrutinized in any of the discussion around the trial of George Zimmerman, but one that relates directly to a discussion I offered in a previous chapter. Advocates of gender justice and feminism believe quite fervently that if we had more women in positions of power, or more women in pretty much everything, the result would be a more just and fair world, either because workplaces and schools would be more equal or because women are inherently predisposed to fairness and justice. Yet the jury at the George Zimmerman trial was an *all-female jury*—not a single man among them—and it seems not to have made any difference whatsoever. As I said earlier, I think we are engaging in an egregious act of self-delusion to think that the world would naturally be better if it were run by women, or the country would naturally be more fair if we had a person of color as president. These aspects of identity are irrelevant—there are good and bad women, fair and unfair women, fair and unfair people of color, fair white women and unfair women of color, and on and on and on. There is no pattern in any of this, and any school of thought that wants me to see what is not in fact there is engaging in a losing battle for the justice they claim to seek.

Yet another element that I discussed earlier comes into play in this moment as well. Not only was the jury all female, but also the jury was all white—with one exception. One of the jurors was of Puerto Rican descent. One does have the civil right in the American justice system to a jury of one's peers, but no one has ever sat down and hammered out exactly what that means. In the Trayvon Martin case, there were many commentators who felt the jury should have been all black, or partly black, or partly Hispanic, or "more diverse," or some other combination of something in order to be considered truly fair (though I never heard anyone say that having all women on a jury in a trial for a man was a problem). It's another example of how we think that diversity is a good thing, even if we are not sure how or why. But the main point I want to make here is that the members of the jury, after the verdict was announced and after the denunciations about how the trial was "clearly racist" had begun, made it clear that in their deliberations, race was not a factor and not something they discussed. They focused, following the instructions of the judge, on the elements of the law.

You might be thinking—Well, okay then, the jury could not possibly be seen as racist in their verdict because they never discussed race. But this is where we have to bring back the perspective of White Studies. In the world of White Studies, white people racially oppress others whenever they talk about race, because they "don't get it," but white people also racially oppress when they *don't* talk about race, because not talking about race is a luxury that only white privilege affords (more on white privilege later). So if the jury did not talk about or consider race in their deliberations, they and the verdict can still be considered racist because when white people don't consider race they are engaging in racism. In other words, no matter what the verdict was, White Studies as a field tells us we can still consider it racist, especially if the jury is (mostly) white and if the victim is non-white. We know that Trayvon Martin was black, so George Zimmerman was made into a "white Hispanic" to allow the White Studies approach to consider him racist, or at least half racist, in his actions. Does it help us obtain justice in this case? Not at all, but it does show just how jaded and stunted our vocabulary has become in discussing issues of diversity and race. It's yet another reason why posturing is what we end up with in these cases, when what we really need is insight and understanding.

Also of interest to note is that the one non-white member of the jury, the woman of Puerto Rican descent who described herself only as "Maddy," agreed to an interview on ABC's *Good Morning America* program with host Robin Roberts. The message she had was that she felt that George Zimmerman had "gotten away with murder" but they could not convict him because they could only consider issues that dealt with the law (which by the way is the exact definition of a fair trial). I think the impression that was intended was that the only woman of color on the jury somehow "got it," even though she said all the jurors struggled with the issues of law (the others were not interviewed), and of course she was interviewed by Robin Roberts because as another woman of color she would "get" what the Puerto Rican juror "got." What concerns me about this way of thinking is that we are talking about a trial, and yet are no longer talking about the law. We are talking about identity, and how identity and thought are paired in immutable ways. The implicit argument here is that if the jury had been filled with women of color, the verdict would have been guilty—as if jurors always vote by identity, regardless of the facts of the case. If diversity worked the way it was supposed to, we would all see how erroneous and damaging this perspective is, wherever it is found.

Trayvon Martin: From justice to identity
Now let's return to the case of Trayvon Martin and to the trial itself and look at how it changed from a question of law to one of identity, and how this transformation completely undermined both fairness and justice. If you are asked a question like, "What do you support, justice or privilege?" then you have been forced into a *posture* that is either one or the other. Supporting Trayvon Martin means demanding a guilty verdict, even before the trial starts, which is somehow seen as justice, and anything else is to side with the *white* Hispanic George Zimmerman, which somehow represents privilege and racism. It is a disaster to think this way because it takes away the ability and the right of anyone to think for themselves about the incident and the case. The issues of law that played out in the court room, ranging from the intricacies of criminal procedure to the specific legal requirements for each of the charges that Zimmerman was facing (such as the distinction between second-degree murder and manslaughter) are here considered secondary if not altogether irrelevant. In the world of *posturing*, you are on one team or the other, on the team of justice or the team of privilege, and this was further qualified by breaking things down into identity-based groups: Team Latino, Team African-American, Team White, and so on, with each group puffing its chest to express its own simplified posture. Embedded in all of this is the absurd idea that identity precedes and determines thought. In the end, *guilty* meant justice, and *not guilty* meant white privilege.

Let me try to break down the elements of this case in brief to show where the disconnect happened. We know that George Zimmerman shot and killed Trayvon Martin. No one, not even

George Zimmerman, has disputed that. George Zimmerman claimed that the act was one of self-defense, a claim that partially draws on Florida's controversial "Stand Your Ground" law (note: it might be a controversial law but it was still in effect as law when the shooting happened). The case went to trial. Prosecutors and defense lawyers had ample time to prepare their cases and to present their arguments. The central question was this: did the killing of Trayvon Martin by George Zimmerman happen in a way that satisfied the legal requirements for a conviction for either second-degree murder or manslaughter? The standard of evidence for this trial, as it is for every trial, is that this must be proven beyond a reasonable doubt. The jurors were clearly instructed on this: if they had any reasonable doubt about any of the evidence—not about whether George Zimmerman killed Trayvon Martin but about whether or not his actions satisfied the legal requirement for the charges—then they were required by law to acquit George Zimmerman. The prosecution failed to present a case that answered those doubts—there were many holes in the prosecution's case—and so the jurors did what they were supposed to do.

Yet after the verdict was announced, we had statements to the effect that this now means it is "open season" on black youth, that anyone with a gun can walk out into the street and shoot an unarmed black youth in a hoodie and walk away with impunity. And that is where the disconnect happened, because those two things are not even remotely linked. There is no open season on black youth. This was not a verdict that said it was okay to shoot and kill a black man under any circumstances. It was a verdict that said the prosecution failed to present a convincing case that George Zimmerman's use of lethal force satisfied the legal requirements for second-degree murder or manslaughter beyond a reasonable doubt. That is all it said, and nothing more.

Nevertheless, the posturing continued and indeed expanded even after the verdict was announced. Rather than study the verdict to determine how it was reached—as I said, the verdict actually made perfect legal sense given the way the case was argued by the prosecution and given the requirements for the jury to reach a guilty verdict—the decision was made to take directly to the streets, much like people do after their team loses a sporting event, to show outrage. "Not guilty" means no justice, with no explanation as to why or how. Protesters marched through cities around the country chanting "No Justice, No Peace," but the demand for justice here meant simply that Zimmerman *had* to be guilty—the meaning and the mechanics of the law apparently meant nothing. This is just empty posturing at its finest, by which I mean at its worst: all of those on Team Justice take to the streets to show how right they are.

This sort of posturing is utterly useless when it comes to dialog and understanding. Not a single person at home was watching the protests and saying: *You know, I thought the verdict was legally valid but now that I saw someone carry a sign, throw a brick through a window, and shout loudly for justice, I think I need to completely reconsider my position.* No one is changing their mind, and the only thing posturing does is act out and dramatize the deep polarization that already exists between identity-based groups. Nothing is changed, nothing is healed, and all you hear are calls from one side to accept things as they are and from the other to keep putting Zimmerman on trial until someone finds him guilty. One of the sad ironies in the middle of all these demands for justice is that demanding a guilty verdict no matter what the evidence proves is actually a violation of one of the foundational elements of civil rights law: that a person is innocent until *proven* guilty in a court of law. The prosecution could not prove beyond a reasonable doubt that George Zimmerman's actions qualified as either second-degree murder or manslaughter, and so he was acquitted. His acquittal is also a part of civil rights, and so if you are marching through the streets demanding civil rights for all, do keep that in mind.

What then do we do? The first thing we need to do is to delink issues of identity from issues of law. I'm not saying they are never related, but it's also the case that they are not *always* related either. Turning the complexities of law into sport or spectacle is not going to produce any better sort of justice for anyone, nor is it going to create a better sense of understanding for how the law works. In the case of George Zimmerman and Trayvon Martin, two people had an encounter that ended tragically. The prosecution had to prove the evidence showed clearly that the encounter met the well-delineated requirements of either second-degree murder or manslaughter *beyond a reasonable doubt.* When the defense was able to show that there was room for reasonable doubt in the case made by the prosecution, the jury was *required by law* to vote not guilty and acquit. That's it. That's all there is to it. By the logic and mechanics of the law, the justice system actually did deliver justice in exactly the way it was supposed to.

Note that accepting the legal logic of the verdict is *not* to condone the law nor is it to betray the idea of justice for Trayvon Martin. The claim that "Trayvon Martin did not deserve to die" is ethically true, and I *fully agree* with that point. But that claim is not a rebuttal of the verdict in the trial, because the question of "Did Trayvon Martin deserve to die?" was not on trial. It's a disconnect created by the confusion of law and ethics. The death of Trayvon Martin was and is a heartbreaking tragedy, one that should never have happened. But we cannot let a misunderstanding of the mechanics of law create or entrench identity-based divisions in American society. Unfortunately, a protest march with signs that say "Better understanding of the law 4 all," or "More legal education in all schools now," or "Critically study the text of the law before rushing to judgment," or even "More qualified prosecuting attorneys in government now"— is a protest that will attract very few people. But posturing is always popular, so "Justice 4 Trayvon" is what we got, with thousands of people marching through the streets with the idea that until some jury somewhere returns a verdict of guilty, "justice" has not occurred.

The airwaves and interwebs were rife with hypotheticals: What if George Zimmerman had been black? What if Trayvon had been white? What if they had both been women? These hypotheticals do nothing except hype up the identity aspects of a case that was never about identity. What if President Obama were a woman? Well, things might be different, but how could I ever prove that? I can't, and no one can. What if Michelle Obama divorced Barack Obama, and Hillary Clinton divorced Bill Clinton, and then Hilary and Michelle got married as a same-sex couple and then ran as co-presidents in 2016? It's an interesting mental exercise, but also pointless. "Justice 4 Trayvon" (I don't know why protesters always feel that the word "for" is too long to write out) cannot possibly mean that we keep dragging George Zimmerman from court to court until we get a guilty verdict of some sort. Legal questions need legal answers. Everything else is extraneous.

Keeping our eyes on the justice prize
What then do we do with the questions of identity that we have? The first thing we need to do is to stop the posturing. Imagine, for instance, the following conversation:

> *Protester*: I fought for change in the justice system after the Trayvon Martin verdict was announced.
> *Passer-by*: Really, what did you do?
> *Protester*: I put on a hoodie and walked through the streets with people who already thought just like me. We held up signs to let each other know we already had the same opinion on the issue.
> *Passer-by*: I see, so what change did that create?
> *Protester*: Well, none. But there were a lot of people there so I know I must be right.

Posturing makes us feel good and announces to like-minded people that we are just like them, but what it doesn't do is create substantive change and more importantly, it completely fails to create a better understanding of ourselves among others. Posturing for approval and affirmation among a crowd of like-minded people does not and never will create "Justice 4 Trayvon."

Now imagine a very different conversation:

Passer-by: Did you walk through the streets last night wearing a hoodie and carrying signs like everyone else?
Advocate for change: No, I realized that it would be a waste of time. Instead I stayed home and read the case and the verdict in detail and realized it made sense by the standards of the law. I disagree with the law itself but understand that the law worked as it was supposed to and the jury did its civic duty properly. I therefore knew that if I wanted to fight to make things better for all I would need to look elsewhere. I re-read Florida's "Stand Your Ground Law" and am thinking of setting up meetings with gun advocacy groups and policymakers to see if there isn't a better way forward for everyone.
Passer-by: That sounds like a lot of work. Wouldn't it just be easier to walk through the streets carrying a simplistic sign?
Advocate for change: Of course it would be easier. That's why it is so popular—no thinking is involved, just posturing. That's also why it accomplishes nothing. I want to create meaningful change and I realize I cannot do that simply by sitting around all day with people who already think like me, constantly telling ourselves how right we are.
Passer-by: You mean, you want to seek out people and groups who think differently from you and try to create understanding, try to persuade them that there might be a better way to do things, a better way to achieve justice?

Advocate for change: Exactly. Sitting around in separate enclaves of people who already think and act alike—posturing, as it is called—does nothing for anyone. "Justice 4 Trayvon" needs to become "Justice for All" and that means I have to actively seek out other groups of people and initiate a dialog for change.

I realize that neither of those dialogs is going to win a Tony award for best drama, but I think the point at least is clear. Issues of justice and issues of diversity will not be resolved or improved by having us all retreat to our separate, homogeneous teams and complain about how the game is unfair. Sometimes the justice system in America *is* unfair—I don't think anyone would admit otherwise. But not every flaw in the justice system is related to an issue of identity, and if we weren't so busy posturing around cases to try to make every trial where the victim and perpetrator are from different identity groups somehow a trial about identity rather than about the law, we would be able to see that more clearly. It's a bit like the way Spike Lee announced in December 2012 that he would boycott Quentin Tarantino's movie *Django Unchained* on the grounds that it did not fit into one of two pre-conceived themes—white oppression or black liberation—that Spike Lee felt had to be at the center of all films about slavery and the black experience in America. It's not like anyone has ever accused Quentin Tarantino of meticulous realism in his films, but in this case Tarantino was at least offering a novel way to re-imagine things that took us outside of the perspectival rut we have been stuck in for so long. Whether it's white oppression or black liberation, or whether it's guilty or not guilty, we need to break free of these tired ways of looking at things. Posturing is simply a form of ideological ossification, a form of preaching to the choir and preaching the same sermon every day, and for anyone who wants a true sense of justice—justice re-imagined as justice for all—we need to walk out of the crowd, walk out of the enclave, reject the posture, dismantle the stereotype, skewer the caricature, and above all else talk across the divides, to make that happen. It's already been too long, and there is precious little time and absolutely no reason to wait any longer.

The false choice of lives that matter
The Trayvon Martin case was of course not an isolated case. In the years since, there has been a sadly long list of similar cases involving the death of young black men. I could go into each of those cases one by one and do the same thing I did with the Trayvon Martin case, which would be to pull apart and separate issues of identity from issues of law, not with the intent to show how they have nothing to do with each other but to show how unproductive it is to assume they are always one and the same. Instead I would like to turn my attention now to the social movement that emerged out of all these tragic cases, to show again how misunderstandings about diversity make us fight the wrong fight, rather than the good fight.

Black Lives Matter emerged in the aftermath of the Trayvon Martin case to create a sustained movement to focus on what appeared to be a rapidly growing number of cases involving police action that resulted in the death of young black men. From a logistical standpoint, the movement has sometimes suffered from a lack of focus—sometimes it's on "racist cops," sometimes on excessive force by police in general (regardless of race), sometimes on social issues within the black community, and sometimes on everything at once. That's not unique to Black Lives Matter either. All large social movements go through logistical struggles and challenges. What I want to focus on instead is how Black Lives Matter has itself become caught up in, and in some ways worsened, the racial divides that threaten continuously to tear America apart. Diversity was supposed to fix those racial divides, but as should be clear to anyone at this point, it hasn't. And again, the reason for diversity's failure is not because we simply need "more diversity" to make it work. It's because we need a different approach to diversity.

If you've spent even two minutes online looking up Black Lives Matter or anything related to it, one of the things you'll come across over and over again in the various exchanges of comments and arguments is the increasingly bitter feud between those who support Black Lives Matter and those who support All Lives Matter. Site after site, article after article, rant after rant, video after video seem almost giddy with delight with each posting of what is ostensibly seen as the "perfect" response to those who advocate All Lives Matter.

The general consensus, based upon everything I've read and watched, seems to be that All Lives Matter is a movement designed to suppress, reject, or undermine Black Lives Matter. Anyone fighting for social justice, especially for the black community in America, therefore had to resist efforts to promote All Lives Matter. Some have gone so far as to claim that All Lives Matter is itself a racist movement, an act of violence against the black community, which leads to the apparent conclusion that if you are opposed to racism, you must also be opposed to All Lives Matter.

I have to say I find this whole debate quite baffling. There's a surprise ending here that we should all take heed of. All Lives Matter and Black Lives Matter are not opposed to each other, and it gravely undermines the struggle for social justice to think that they are. Not only do you not have to choose between the two, as if they were mutually exclusive ideas, but also, and more importantly, you actually can't support one without also supporting the other. As it turns out, they're inseparable.

While All Lives Matter and Black Lives Matter may be inseparable, that doesn't mean they are the same thing. They do have a few important differences. All Lives Matter, for instance, is a movement of *non-discrimination*. The principle of non-discrimination is actually a fundamental pillar of human rights, so to dismiss All Lives Matter is also to dismiss human rights, which is not something you want to dismiss in a fight for social justice. The principle of non-discrimination does not say, as so many people seem to think, that we should care equally about all people in all situations, regardless of context. What it says is that when action is required, or assistance is needed, we must care equally *for all of those in need* without discrimination. If a country offers free health care, for instance, it can certainly differentiate the sick from the healthy, and can even differentiate citizen from non-citizen. Neither of those is considered discrimination from a human rights standpoint. But what that country cannot do is offer free health care to some groups but deny it to others, based solely on specific elements of their identity. That would be discrimination.

Black Lives Matter, by contrast, is a movement of *prioritization*. It says that right now, the various crises that affect the black community in the United States require our undivided attention and should also receive first priority. Hands down, the most common refrain I come across when I read the various exchanges between the two movements is, "How can #AllLivesMatter until #BlackLivesMatter?" (or some variation thereof). What this really comes down to is the question of triage, a term borrowed from the medical profession that refers to the prioritization of patients based on the severity of their injuries. From a human rights perspective, triage is not considered an act of discrimination, so on that front, Black Lives Matter is certainly an acceptable perspective to advocate.

Where Black Lives Matter stumbles, however, is in its insistence on absolute prioritization. If you think of a hospital emergency room, where ten people show up all at the same time, the medical staff can certainly prioritize those who need medical assistance right away—those with life-threatening injuries, for instance—over those whose injuries and ailments are less severe. What they cannot do is treat *only* those with life-threatening injuries—they can prioritize, but they still must care for all ten people because all ten have a right to equal consideration and care. The most severely injured can get higher priority (Black Lives Matter), but they cannot have absolute priority—all those who need medical help have a right to receive it, too (All Lives Matter).

Nevertheless, all over the internet and all over social media, post after post talks about the "perfect refutation" of All Lives Matter, as if to validate Black Lives Matter as the only acceptable perspective to hold. One of these perfect refutations involves a short, three-frame cartoon.[8] It's worth a walk-through to see how this debate is really a false debate based on a false choice.

The first frame shows a person with a rather smug expression insisting that *all* lives matter. It is a complete misrepresentation of the issue as an either/or choice. All Lives Matter is not a negative retort to Black Lives Matter, as if to say, "Are you saying your black life is more important than mine?" All Lives Matter is saying that all lives deserve equal value and consideration, so a black life should matter as much as a white life or any other life. If there is a discrepancy, then there is a problem. In that sense, any person advocating an All Lives Matter perspective must necessarily support a Black Lives Matter perspective as well. They move in the same direction—each supports the other.

The second frame has the same smug character, holding a garden hose, saying that "we should care exactly equally at all times about everything." Again, this is a complete misrepresentation of what *non-discrimination* is. Non-discrimination does not say that we give exactly the same consideration to everything and everyone at all times, regardless of context. It says that when action is required or assistance is needed, we must perform such action or render such assistance *to all who are in need* without discrimination. As with my example of triage above, differentiating between those who are

---

[8] To view the cartoon, see German Lopez, "Next time someone tells you "all lives matter," show them this cartoon," *Vox* (July 11, 2016) at https://www.vox.com/2015/9/4/9258133/white-lives-matter

in urgent need of assistance and those who are not does not violate the principle of non-discrimination.

The third frame shows why this issue is presented as a false choice. The smug man with the garden hose is pouring water on his own house, which is fine, while next door a house is on fire. "All houses matter," says the man. But a house on fire and a house that is not are clearly not the same thing, and only a complete idiot would think they deserve equal consideration. That is not what an All Lives Matter perspective advocates—not even close. We can and must differentiate between a house that is on fire and one that is not—clearly the house on fire is the one in need of assistance, and so we rightfully *prioritize* the house on fire. Non-discrimination does not say that the house that is not on fire deserves equal care and consideration. What non-discrimination says is that we must render assistance to the house that is on fire regardless of whose house it is.

So the cartoon presents not a perfect response, but a perfect display of ignorance in action, a complete misrepresentation of the issue that serves only to divide us further. A better version would add a fourth frame, where we see that there are many houses on fire. If we accept the premise of the cartoon that the burning house represents the black community, what would we do in a situation where the black house was on fire, but so, too, were the Latino house, the LGBTQI+ house, the Asian house, the women's house, and so forth? If we accept the Black Lives Matter perspective, and reject the All Lives Matter perspective, then our only concern would be the black house, and we would leave all the other houses to burn to the ground. That's hardly a recipe for justice.

How sad is it that two movements asking us to care more for others have somehow managed to make us fight with each other instead? All Lives Matter and Black Lives Matter are not mutually exclusive movements, and one is not a refutation or a denial of the other. They move in the same direction and they are fundamentally inseparable—there is really no way to support one without also supporting the other.

Consider this hypothetical situation: If a black man is driving home and sees a severely injured Latina on the side of the road, should he stop to help? If we accept the premise that all lives cannot matter *until* black lives matter, then he would drive past and leave the Latina to die. He'll only stop if he sees a black life in trouble, because black lives matter and that should be our only priority right now. However, if we instead accept the premise that black lives matter *because* all lives matter, then he will stop to help. In stopping to render help, he does not in that moment stop caring about black people. Nor is he saying, as so many people have inanely suggested, that the lives of uninjured people somehow don't matter or matter less than the lives of those who are injured.

So don't be fooled—there's no choice to be made here. It's a disgrace that we are fighting over things like how much empathy and compassion we should have and to whom we should offer it. If we start doing the work of diversity the right way, there should be plenty of empathy and compassion to go around. Wherever there's a house on fire, I'll be there to help. Hope to see you there, too.

CHAPTER 3

CONFRONTING DIVERSITY

I have said right from the start of this whole series about ourselves among others that racism is far more prevalent than we care to admit. Fortified with lies and delusions about how only dominant groups can be racist, or more specifically, about how racism is what whites do to every other group, or about how empowering non-dominant identity groups automatically resists racism, we continue to fight a battle that was already lost before it started. The only way to defeat racism is to fight racism wherever and whenever it occurs. If we haven't made better progress in the fight against racism so far, it isn't because we haven't tried and it certainly isn't because "white racism" is so deeply entrenched that we have to fight still harder. It is because we are only fighting a small part of the problem, and the reason we are only fighting a small part of the problem is because we have intentionally blinded ourselves to the prevalence of racism because we cannot reconcile the existence of a multi-racial racism with the simplistic ideas we currently hold about diversity. If you want to fight for social justice, if you want to fight racism, if you want to fight to create a diversity that works equally for all, then you will have to take the painful first step toward acknowledging that racism is everywhere and it comes from every direction. Anyone and everyone can be racist, and all too often, people are. Let the confrontations begin.

Confronting the new face of racism
Racism is, among other things, an act of exclusion, so let me start with an example of how the exclusionary impulse can come up with very little effort from any direction. One of the exercises I do in my classes from time to time starts with a simple question. I vary the identity in question each time I do this, but for now I will use the identity-category of Latino. The way the exercise works is this: I walk into the class and I tell my students I woke up that morning with the clarity and resolve to know exactly what I wanted to be in life, and when they look on with anticipation to know what that is, I say with as much enthusiasm as I can muster—I want to be Latino. Suddenly the anticipation of the students turns to laughter, which then becomes nervous laughter. The first part of the laughter is because the idea seems impossibly absurd. The nervous laughter starts when they realize I might actually be serious. What I then do is ask the students what I would need to do be become Latino, and more importantly, what I would need to do to be accepted by others as Latino. At first, a few simple things are offered as "requirements." I would need to speak Spanish—I can do that, so no problem. Someone will usually say I have to dress a certain way, but when I press the issue and ask how Latinos dress, no one can come up with any one particular way of dressing that defines a Latino, so that gets dropped. Someone will usually say that I need to learn Latino history, food, and culture—that I know, so no problem there either. The exercise gets harder and harder as students struggle to figure out what exactly makes someone Latino. At some point, students realize they have shifted their focus away from how I *can* become Latino to how I *cannot* be Latino, even if I wanted to. The effort is now exerted on finding ways to *exclude* me, rather than include me. In other words, discrimination quickly

becomes the operative norm, even as students are quite unaware they are doing it. Eventually—and this is almost always the case when there is someone in the class from the identity-group I have used for the exercise (in this case, Latino)—someone will say that I cannot be Latino because I am just "too different." No matter how hard I try, I just won't be accepted as Latino. Especially by other Latinos.

Others will offer the argument that someone has to be "born Latino" to be Latino, and since I wasn't born Latino, I can't be Latino. Ever. Again, I press a bit further and ask about purity of identity. What percentage of a person has to be Latino before they can be accepted as "authentically" Latino? As I pointed out in an earlier chapter, DNA tests have become quite popular, with some people going so far as to change their whole identity based on DNA they didn't know they had. So is a person only Latino if they are 100% "pure" Latino? And if not, then what is the DNA cut-off for authenticity? If I take a DNA test and learn that I am 46% Latino, is that "close but not quite"? Students struggle to find a cut-off point, and no matter how many times I have done this exercise, no convincing answer has ever been offered. And if you are thinking that the answer should be 100%, I can all but guarantee that if you started doing DNA tests, you'd be hard-pressed to find anyone on earth who is 100% Latino.

I might then push the issue in a different direction. What does it mean to say I am "too different"? Is it because I look white? And if that is the case, what color are Latinos and are they all the same color? Sometimes just for fun I will ask if I am "white like Charlie Sheen?" and when some students say "yes!" I remind them that Charlie Sheen is actually from a Latino family. Confusion sets in. Things get uncomfortable. I might even ask for confirmation: "So you are saying that no matter how hard I try—being fluent in Spanish, knowing all of Latino history and food and culture, living in a Latino neighborhood, dressing and acting Latino, and doing pretty much everything you suggested I need to do to be Latino—no matter how hard I try and what I do, I cannot be Latino?" Most students will reluctantly confirm that this is true.

Then I shift the question a bit. Okay, so what if I want to become Mexican? The obvious answers come up first—I'd have to move to Mexico, take Mexican citizenship, give up my American citizenship, speak Spanish, and so forth. I could easily do all of that, so assuming I have done all of that, at that point am I considered Mexican? Students will scramble for an answer, though at this point the answer is still usually no. So when, I ask, at what specific point, would people see me and accept me as Mexican? The answers I get are interesting. One student said only when I can speak Spanish fluently and without an accent could I be truly Mexican. Another said I would have to give up "American things," and when I asked what that meant, she clarified that I would have to watch Mexican TV shows, listen to Mexican music, follow Mexican sports, participate in Mexican politics, and so forth. There does seem to be more agreement on this part of the exercise, however, that at some point, after an awful lot of effort and transformation, I could eventually be Mexican. Once that point is established, I then follow up with this question: "But aren't Mexicans considered Latinos?"

At some point I might bring in a question like this: "So, what if I don't speak a word of Spanish, don't know a thing about Latino culture or history or food, have no Latino friends, grew up in northern Maine, but my last name is Morales—then I am Latino?" The answer here is a surprisingly easy yes. In other words, no matter how hard I struggle to adopt the ways of the Latino community, no matter how hard I try to assimilate to the community and interact with everyone in the community, I will always be eyed with suspicion, and I will always be rendered a perpetual outsider, no matter how hard I try to fit in. Yet if I know nothing of Latino life and culture, but have a Latino name—suddenly I'm in.

I eventually bring the discussion back to diversity in America. I will take the standards we just established regarding my effort to acquire an identity and apply them to America in general. "So if someone comes to the United States from another country," I might ask, "and they become a citizen and know everything about American culture and food, but somehow they appear "different," then is it okay to say that no matter how hard they try they can never be accepted as American?" Remember, one student told me I could only be Mexican if I spoke Spanish fluently and without an accent, so applying that standard here in America, it would mean that anyone in America who spoke English with an accent or less-than-fluently would, by the student's own standard, not be truly American.

The point of the exercise, of course, is not just to highlight the arbitrariness of identity boundaries, but also to point out how diversity makes us blind to our own discriminatory actions and beliefs, even as we clearly see them in others. Building walls and engaging in cultural "gatekeeping"—the act of accepting or rejecting people from a category of existence—is something that all groups tend to do. Whether a group is dominant or non-dominant is irrelevant. What is central is the act of exclusion. *It is the act of exclusion that is the problem, not the identity of the group doing the excluding.* People often complain that America is "so racist" because it is slow to recognize (for instance) a Korean-American as American, yet when that same Korean-American is asked the question of whether I could ever be Korean, they have no problem saying they simply could never accept me as Korean (and I've done this exercise using "Korean" rather than "Latino," and to date, no Korean has ever said they could see me as Korean, no matter what I do). I would accept the premise that diversity is supposed to make us more aware of how exclusion of others among ourselves is an act of discrimination and therefore wrong, but we need to accept that premise as equally binding on all groups, and not just on one.

In other words, the "perpetual foreigner" complaint that is often heard from different identity-groups in America is really something that is common to all groups. The sad reality is that when we get used to spending too much time among ourselves we tend to exclude others, often automatically, usually arbitrarily, and sometimes even violently. Diversity as a practice should not reward us for "sticking with our own kind," nor should it force us to float free as disconnected individuals with no meaningful connections to anyone else. What diversity should be doing is encouraging us to discard those identities that are inherently exclusionary and create new ones that are inherently inclusionary. Part of that process is to identify and "out" the many ways that exclusion happens in American society, far beyond the haplessly simplistic notion that exclusion is something that the dominant majority does to everyone else. We like to use words like "inclusivity" when we speak of diversity, yet the groups who advocate most vociferously for diversity are themselves often formed from the most exclusionary of groups. We need to do something new and different. In short, we need to have the strength and integrity to identify what I would call *the new face of racism*. We'll have to put up with some discomfort in the short run to get to a sense of justice in the long run, but there's really no other way around it.

Meet Frederic Nottebohm
If you think my whole tale of "becoming Latino" was just one more classroom exercise with little attachment to the real world, then I suppose it's time to introduce you to Frederic Nottebohm. You've probably never heard of him, unless you went to law school and studied international law, but Nottebohm's name is attached to what many people in the legal profession see as the key definitive legal precedent for determining "true" national identity. The case came before the International Court of Justice (ICJ), the court attached to the United Nations, in 1955, and the question at hand

was whether Nottebohm was who said he was and who his country said he was.[9]

First, let's look at the facts of the case. Nottebohm was born in Germany in 1881 and was a German citizen. As a young man, he moved to Guatemala and went into business with his brothers, creating a firm known as *Los Nottebohm Hermanos* (not to be confused with *Los Pollos Hermanos*). Though he lived in and conducted business in Guatemala for 34 years, he never applied for Guatemalan citizenship and retained his German citizenship. At the start of World War II, due to business restrictions against Germany and German citizens by both the United States and Guatemala, Nottebohm found that he could no longer do business in Guatemala and, having left Guatemala, was not allowed to return. Nottebohm subsequently applied for and received citizenship in Liechtenstein, where one of his brothers lived, in 1939, and renounced his German citizenship. Liechtenstein was a neutral country, and thus was not subject to the same sanctions and restrictions as Germany (a belligerent country) in Guatemala. Nottebohm then tried to return to Guatemala but Guatemala refused to recognize his new identity, denying Nottebohm entry and refusing him access to his property and affairs. Eventually Guatemalan authorities confiscated his property and assets, and Nottebohm was now suing to get them back.

The ICJ cannot hear cases from individuals—its jurisdiction extends only to state-to-state legal disputes. As a result, Liechtenstein represented Nottebohm in a contentious case against Guatemala, coming to the defense of one of its citizens against the actions of Guatemala. Liechtenstein argued to the court that they regarded Nottebohm as a citizen of Liechtenstein, and presented their case by arguing that he had done everything legally necessary and

---

[9] The full text of the court's decision can be found at http://www.icj-cij.org/files/case-related/18/018-19550406-JUD-01-00-EN.pdf

proper according to the process of naturalization in Liechtenstein. They regarded Nottebohm as one of their own, and they had the legal papers to prove it.

Guatemala argued on the other hand that Nottebohm was not "really" a Liechtensteiner. They argued that Nottebohm acquired his new citizenship simply to take advantage of the opportunities it provided and to find a convenient way to continue to make money in Guatemala. The lawyers for Guatemala argued that citizenship was based on more than just law and physical residence. Guatemala argued that citizenship required assimilation to the traditions and culture of a country, and a clear display that the interests of the country of citizenship came before the interests of any other country. Guatemala argued that Nottebohm continued to speak German, had gone to Germany on a regular basis to visit family, and showed no significant or emotional attachment to Liechtenstein. In essence, because Nottebohm continued to practice and follow the culture and traditions of his home country, and to visit there as well, he could not be considered a true Liechtensteiner. Thus, Guatemala did not have to recognize the identity he professed, and did not owe him any compensation for his property or assets.

The ICJ sided with Guatemala, stating that Nottebohm had not shown clear evidence, with regard to Liechtenstein, of becoming sufficiently "wedded to its traditions, its interests, its way of life" to be regarded as an authentic Liechtensteiner. This is spite of the fact that Liechtenstein itself said he was. In other words, if you acquire the citizenship of a country, but (1) continue to have emotional and physical ties to your former country, including to its culture and traditions and apparently even extending to family visits, and (2) do not become sufficiently "wedded' (the ICJ's exact word) to the culture and traditions of the new country, it is acceptable to see you as not "really" belonging to the country of your newly-acquired citizenship.

Mine, yours, ours: redefining racism
What, then, is the new face of racism? The old way of looking at racism was, as I talked about at length earlier, to claim that racism was something that only the dominant group can do because racism had to be based on power, and only the dominant group had power, and so presto—if we just fight the dominant group and dismantle their power, then we also dismantle racism. The new face of racism is based on the realization that this original formulation of racism is absurd. If we change the definition of racism toward something more general and something that applies to all rather than just to some, we get a whole new chance to finally defeat the ugly and persistent social cancer of racism. So, how about something more general for a definition of what racism is, in the hope that we can get started on eliminating racism together? Here's my new definition of racism, to help get the anti-racist ball rolling:

> *Racism occurs when any individual or group acts or encourages others to think or behave in negative or disparaging ways that employ exclusionary categories of racial identity.*

It might not be perfect, but at least it's a place to start. We can easily extend it to other group-based identities as well, such as ethnicity, so it does have some versatility.

Consider the standard scenario of racism, the kind you might see in any Hollywood film about racism. A bunch of redneck white boys pull up to the house of a black family and throw a brick through the window with a message of "Get out!" (or they burn the house or they burn a cross in the yard or they do all sorts of other horrible things…there's quite sadly a very long menu of racist actions to choose from). Does that fit the definition of racism I just offered? Indeed it does—quite easily, in fact, so that's covered.

But now let's look at a few other things that are less extreme or less obvious, to see how they might also be construed as racism, given this newer and all-inclusive definition (and remember, diversity is all about inclusion). Suppose you are sitting in a meeting and someone keeps going on about "My people..." or "the fight for rights and justice for my people..." and so on. Given the exercise I described, let's say this person is Latino and he is a self-proclaimed leader of "his people" (by which I mean he sees himself as a leader, even if others don't). Now me, I support justice for all people, so perhaps I would want to join in this struggle. So if I ask this person whether I can join in, and he replies "no, White people are the problem," then because he is advocating a view that thinks in terms of exclusion and negative characterization by racial identity, I would rightfully see this person as racist. Diversity advocates in the present might see it as "empowerment" or "community building," and so forth, but I think justice is better served if we start seeing it as racism. We need to start breaking down these narratives of homogeneity ("Latinos only") and normativity ("Latinos should vote/think/act this way") that stand in the way of mutual and meaningful understanding of ourselves among others. *Anyone who wants to divide us in any exclusionary way is working against the premise and the promise of diversity.*

Let's take a simple phrase and rework it a bit to see how redefining racism helps us put diversity back onto equally shared ground. Suppose a white person made the claim, "I don't feel comfortable around black people." Is that a racist statement? Absolutely. But let's look at *why* it's a racist statement. The first thing it does is call attention to exclusionary racial identities. That certainly satisfies one part of our new definition of racism. The second thing it does is make a negative assessment about black people that encourages us to think negatively about black people. That satisfies the second part of the new definition, and thus we end up with the conclusion that it is a racist statement.

Now let's take a similar statement, with one key revision. Suppose a black person made the claim, "I don't feel comfortable around white people." With our current definition of racism, we couldn't consider that a racist statement on the grounds that black people can't be racist. If we engage the new definition of racism, however, we get a different result. Why? For the exact same reasons as the first statement, that's why. It calls attention to exclusionary racial identities, and it makes a negative assessment about white people that encourages us to think negatively about white people. At this point, of course, someone will try to point out that the two statements aren't the same because white people oppress others merely by existing, whereas black people, as persons of color, are incapable of doing so. Yet if we can't ask whether the white person making a negative statement about blacks has any compelling or legitimate reason for their antipathy, the principle of equality—and diversity is all about equality—says that we can't ask the question of the black person either. We remove the power element from the definition of racism and instead focus on the *intent*. If the intent is to make us think racially in terms of exclusion and disparagement, then it's racism, regardless of who made the comment. That creates equality of responsibility for all of us, which is the only way we have a chance at finally ending racism once and for all.

From exclusion to inclusion
Imagine a campus where there is a meeting of, say, the Korean Student Association (which includes both students from Korea and Korean-Americans). It's the first week of the semester, and so students are looking for new things to do and new activities to participate in, student groups being one such possibility. But now let's imagine something different happens this time around. Suppose at that first meeting of the semester, a truly diverse group of students how up: Latinos, Chinese and Japanese students (including Chinese-American and Japanese-American), Whites, Africans and

African-Americans—anyone interested in knowing Korean students. How do think that would play out? If the situation becomes one of "sorry, this is for Korean students only," then people should walk away and denounce the group as racist (using our new definition of racism). So how do we resolve the situation and eliminate racism? We invite everyone to stay at the meeting and join the organization. Maybe it's time to stop having groups that are exclusionary and completely rethink how we might organize ourselves among others. Instead of a Korean Student Association, how about the Association for All Students Interested in Korea? Just a thought.

I have one final example to show how our confused and inadequate ideas of what diversity is end up replicating the problems we are supposedly trying to overcome. We will never defeat racism if we only look at one part of the problem. A few years ago, UC Berkeley had an event on campus to fight for the rights of "people of color" (and again, everyone has a color, so the category of people of color should include everyone, though it doesn't). I remember the poster for the start of the campaign on campus because it had a prominent piece of artwork, a drawing actually, that showed people of color coming together—all of them depicted in cultural clothing from different parts of the world even though this was a movement only for people of color in America—under the slogan, "The Twenty-First Century Will Be Ours!" As far as I am concerned, if the twenty-first century belongs to you, and I am not a part of that, then all you are really doing is replacing one racism with another. A movement that confuses justice with the idea of vengeance—"you excluded me so I cannot wait to get the chance to replicate that and do the same thing back to you"—is a movement that is as useless as it is offensive. We'll have to do better than that to get to a diversity that works for all. It's time to have the courage to identify racism wherever and whenever it occurs, no matter what color or variety or form it comes in, and to take a collective stand against it.

Post-racial America and other misconceptions
One of the big buzzwords—more of a phrase actually— that came into circulation in the aftermath of President Obama's election in 2008 was the idea of a "post-racial America." Now that we had a black president, race no longer mattered, some argued, or at least race was no longer an obstacle or a problem. America had moved on to new territory, new formulations of identity that made race irrelevant. Diversity had finally been achieved. There was no shortage of critics and skeptics of course, some who argued that race was still very much a problem in America, others who argued that the whole idea of a "post-racial America" was a trick by the dominant group to disempower communities of color. Still others argued that it was a nice idea but will take a lot more work to make it happen.

The reality is that we do not live in a post-racial America. It is hard to argue that post-racial America started with a black president (emphasizing race as part of his identity) or that government has paved the way for helping us move beyond race when we still have things like the Congressional Black Caucus or the California Latino Legislative Caucus and all sorts of other groups of politicians and policy makers who still think that race is a useful and constructive lens through which to view and craft law and policy. I personally don't like the idea of a "post-racial America" for the same reason I am opposed to our current understandings of diversity: it is a passive process and not an active one. If we are "post-racial" right now—and we aren't—it is because it just somehow happened along the way, we woke up one morning and said "hey, I didn't think about race today—I guess somehow we all became post-racial." It's as meaningless a concept as someone saying, "hey, I'm Asian and not white, so I guess I have diversity." Things like that don't and can't just happen passively—we have to *make* them happen, willfully and actively, and in the process of making them happen we give them both direction and meaning.

What I would suggest instead is that we become not a post-racial America, but an *anti-racial America*. What is an anti-racial America, you ask? An anti-racial America is one that moves beyond the old and simplistic idea of "fighting the white man" and instead learns to identify the new face of racism—a face that is truly diverse—and to stand opposed to it wherever and whenever it occurs. We need to be vigilant of all of the ways that race, and along with it all forms of exclusionary and divisive identities, are manipulated to create or perpetuate acts of discrimination and perspectives of prejudice. And more than just being vigilant is the need to stand united against them. It's the only way to make racism a part of the past. Even then, the idea of a post-racial America might be a pipe dream at best. A post-racial America is a lot like diversity: it is not something that is achieved, but rather something that is continuously cultivated and practiced, an ideal that we continuously strive for and aspire to. It is also something that is fragile and ephemeral. So even if today appears to be a post-racial day, there is always the possibility that tomorrow will be an ugly relapse, and so the work is never done. But as I have continuously said, while the work of diversity is hard work and it is endless work, it is also good work. We may not ever get to the endpoint of a world without racism or a world with perfect diversity, but any effort in that direction can't help but make things better.

Joining the race for the diversity winner's circle
For a recent example of the sort of deranged thinking that our current views on diversity both produce and accept, one need look no further than the relatively recent book by Amy Chua called *The Triple Package* (2013). In this book, several cultural/religious/ethnic groups are identified as having the "right" values and the "right" cultural practices to succeed (success being measured as acquiring money and status). Those that didn't make the cut, such as African-Americans, were apparently just defective cultures,

destined for a lack of success. There is much to quibble with in the book, such as the fact while Chinese-Americans are singled out as successful, Japanese-Americans and Korean-Americans are either assumed to be Chinese or are left out as inferior imitations of the "true" Asian culture of China (no surprise, Amy Chua is Chinese-American).

What I want to focus on here, however, in relation to this book (and there are many books like it), are the consequences of what this sort of thinking does for diversity in America. Even if the premise were true—that identity-based groups that have a sense of superiority, insecurity, and impulse control (the "triple package") are simply bound for success in a way that other, presumably inferior cultures are not—the premise encourages us, indeed requires us, to think by race, to act by race, and not just stay in our own separate enclaves but also build up the boundaries around them to keep the other cultural riff-raff out, lest they dilute our success-generating values. It creates little more than a slightly-revised version of apartheid. In apartheid-era South Africa, the white minority that ruled the country argued that race was a sort of, well, race, and the results were in and whites came in first. Whites came in first because they had the best values—intelligence, civilization, and so forth—and therefore were destined to rule. Strict laws against mixing races together were put in place to prevent any threats to racial purity, because in the genetic lottery, some groups had been blessed with success and some groups hadn't—the former were destined to rule and the latter were destined to be ruled by others. One side-note to all of this: individuals that like to set up hierarchies among racial and cultural groups will always create hierarchies that put themselves at the top. No surprise that Amy Chua, a Chinese-American woman, and Jed Rubenfeld, a Jewish-American man (the book is co-authored), put their own identity groups in the winners' circle. Ironic, too, since I consider the entire project an epic fail.

But back to diversity. Here is a book that says: if you belong to one of the lucky groups, then by all means stay in your group—stick to your own kind—and more importantly, build up the walls to keep others out. This is the recipe for success. It is an idea that sets us back a century in terms of diversity and inter-cultural understanding. Indeed, it is a book that all but says we should stop trying to attain diversity, since the jury has already ruled and has told us which groups are winners and which groups are losers. Let's all move to the enclave and then build a wall—separate but unequal. The only possibility for change is for the non-dominant loser groups to assimilate to the dominant winner groups. Should the African-American man pray that he finds a Chinese wife, so that his child can have at least half a chance to succeed in life? Should the Chinese woman reject the proposal from the African-American man, lest it drag her child's chances for success down by half? The point is, the whole project encourages us to think by group, to think narcissistically by group, to think selfishly by group, and lost in all of it is the possibility of mutual understanding. Without mutual understanding, diversity has no chance of success.

Also lost in all of this is the individual, who is now sacrificed to the stereotypical norms of his or her group. From my perspective, I would be far more impressed by a Puerto Rican child growing up in a gang-ridden and drug-infused urban nightmare who single-handedly negotiated every threat and temptation to make it into a local community college than by the son of a wealthy Mormon family who used the family's exclusive community network to get into Harvard. The central point of the American Dream is that we can break-free of lineage-based destiny, monarchy being the most extreme example of that (which incidentally was the generative moment of the American Revolution, to fight against the idea that some jackass born into a particular family had a right to rule others merely by virtue of his or her birth). Whether it is royal families or superior ethnic groups, the premise is garbage. I've met a lot of stupid Mormons and I've met a lot of brilliant Puerto Ricans. *In an anti-racist America,* we need to resist the call to see them as "exceptions" to the inescapable group rule, and see them for the individuals they are. When we try to separate American society into group winners and group losers, the reality is that no one wins, and we all lose badly.

Why white privilege exists and why it doesn't
Speaking of group rules, it's finally time to confront head on this thing known as "White Privilege." White Privilege, as its name suggests, refers to the untold privileges that the dominant group of America grants to itself and denies to all others. It is not something that whites can opt out of or renounce, rather it is only something that whites can acknowledge and accept. Complicity is assumed, and guilt is presumed. Whites earn these privileges by birth, which means they are unearned and presumably therefore undeserved, and whites retain those privileges for themselves because they control the unwritten rules of American society, rules which they created to protect and preserve their privilege. Since all whites possess and enjoy white privilege merely by virtue of existence, all whites, whether they know it or not, are inherently oppressive and discriminatory. For a white person to deny they have white privilege is only to exacerbate the situation. The only thing more oppressive than a white person is a white person who denies they oppress.

Non-whites, or people of color, on the other hand, experience only discrimination, which is the negative corollary to white privilege. Whites oppress, so by definition and design, non-whites are oppressed. The problem here, as it is commonly argued, is that whites are so immersed in their privilege that they are not even conscious of that privilege, which means that whites oppress without even being aware of it. Whites unconsciously oppress non-whites, so as a sort of "consciousness-raising" form of diversity activism, non-white groups have exerted tremendous effort to make whites conscious of their inherently oppressive ways, giving rise to admonitions such as "check your privilege." When a person of color tells a white person to "check their privilege," it means the white person is doing something or saying something that reveals their lack of awareness of the privilege they are enjoying in that moment.

To give an example of the sort of context in which this might occur, I can share an anecdote from one of my students, who was in another class (not my class) that was part of what is called the American Cultures curriculum. This is a curriculum in which certain classes are given the "American Cultures" designation because they offer special insights into American culture and society. During a lecture on race in America, my student, who is white, raised her hand to make a comment. When she began to offer her comment, however, she was cut-off by an African-American student who told her that whites don't have the right to talk about race. When my student tried again to make her comment, the same student cut her off, this time with the phrase "check your privilege." The idea here is that a white person cannot talk about race because their white privilege prevents them from having any understanding of what racism is, since they are only capable of being racist and not of experiencing racism.

I'm not going to wade into the heady debate on whether or not white privilege actually exists. That would take a separate book. Rather I am going to take a different tack here by focusing on why some people need to *believe* that white privilege exists. You may have heard the argument, for example, that the concept of race is really just a social construct. What that means is that race does not really exist, it has no substance in and of itself, but at some point in time people needed to believe race existed because it served a useful purpose for their needs. White Europeans needed a concept with which to interpret and evaluate perceived social difference,

Unpoisoning the Well

and the concept that fit that conceptual need was the concept of race. The question of whether race was real or not became irrelevant. What mattered is that people believed it was real, and they believed it was real because it served a purpose that furthered their interests or provided some tangible benefit to the group that believed in the concept.

I mention this because white privilege, which is itself based on the social construct of race, is itself a social construct. Proving whether white privilege is real or not is not the issue here any more than proving whether race is real or not. What matters is that people need to believe that white privilege exists because it furthers their interests or provides them with a tangible benefit. As with the concept of race, the important question to ask here is not whether white privilege exists but rather what purpose it serves for those people who believe it exists. Race was constructed in its historical moment to explain perceived social disparities in ways that were hierarchical and biological, because to use race in this way allowed those who invented the concept to consider themselves superior and mask social discrimination as a scientific imperative. So why was white privilege constructed? What purpose does its construction serve? For starters, in its historical moment, it defines oppression in ways that automatically exempt its presumed victims (similar to defining racism in ways that exempt people of color), and it reduces the complexity of oppression by focusing responsibility on one group only, thereby exempting all others from responsibility.

As with race, pointing out that white privilege is a social construct doesn't necessarily alleviate the situation or end the problem. As long as those who believe in the social construct obtain utility or benefit from believing in the concept, they will continue to dismiss whatever evidence someone might offer to the contrary as "fake news" or something like it. A more constructive tactic in this situation, one that also works with race, is to point out the absurdities and contradictions that accrue when we take white privilege as a social fact rather than a social construct. And that I will do with a little thing I like to call *privilege laundering*.

Privilege laundering
It's easier to show what privilege laundering is by example than it is to define it, but I suppose it would be disingenuous to evade the effort to explain the concept in clear terms. In a nutshell, privilege laundering refers to the way that non-white privilege, which by the definition of white privilege cannot exist, is erased or transformed into something that reconciles with the original social construct of white privilege. Non-white privilege, like drug money in the open economy, would be considered illicit and illegitimate by the rules of the original social construct, so what is needed is a way to launder privilege into oppression.

So, let's start with an example. In Colombia, there has been a rising tide of complaints over the past several years from Afro-Colombians—Colombians of African descent—who claim that they are consistently denied entrance into various venues in Bogotá simply because they are black.[10] The denial of entry was really just a flashpoint for broader and more systemic claims of racism that Afro-Colombians have faced on a continuous basis. Interestingly, the perpetrators of these acts of racism, which are well-documented, are often referred to in the Colombian context as white (*raza blanca*), but in this case white refers *not* to American or European expats living in Bogotá, but to Colombian owners of these venues, people who would be referred to in any other context as Latino/a.[11]

---

10 Norbey Quevedo Hernández, "El bar que no acepta negros," *El Espectador* (June 11, 2016) at http://www.elespectador.com/noticias/investigacion/el-bar-no-acepta-negros-articulo-637237

11 Hernando Salazar, "Discriminación por raza en bares de Bogotá," *Semana* (October 18, 2008) at http://www.semana.com/noticias/articulo/discrimina-

If racial oppression can only happen because one group is dominant and therefore privileged, then what we have here is a clear example of Latino privilege.

If we want to cling to our mistaken belief that only whites can be privileged, if we want to uphold the social construct for what it is, then consider this unpalatable outcome. A nightclub owner in Colombia spends the evening denying blacks entrance to his nightclub—one racist act after another, all night long.[12] After he closes up his venue, he heads to the airport and boards a flight to San Francisco. He arrives at SFO after a long flight and then, as he leaves the plane and steps into the cool air of the city, something amazing happens: his privilege magically disappears. It has been laundered. The man who spent the prior evening engaging in egregious acts of racism is now himself a victim. During the flight he was absolved of all crimes. As he exits the plane he is now considered incapable of racism, never a perpetrator and always a victim. Privilege has been laundered into oppression. And yet we wonder why our efforts to end racism are ineffective.

If that scenario isn't quite enough for you, I'll offer another. This one happened in India while I was living there a few years ago. I don't have time to go into all the intricacies and complexities of the caste system in India, but for this scenario, just understand that in the construction of caste hierarchy, Brahmins are considered the most pure and are therefore at the top of the hierarchy, and Dalits are considered to be the most polluted (or completely impure) and are therefore at the bottom of the hierarchy—so low in fact that technically they are below the hierarchy itself. Also understand that food and water can "transfer" impurities from one person to another if they are shared.

---

cion-raza-bares-bogota/96404-3

12 Mónica Cabarcas, "¿Son racistas estos bares?" *SoHo* (June 2005) at http://www.soho.co/historias/articulo/son-racistas-estos-bares/5269

In Tamil Nadu, a state in southern India with a relatively large population of Dalits, the government had been actively enforcing new regulations regarding caste reservations, which reserve seats in classrooms and other places for groups normally excluded from them (such as Dalits). It was in this context that a young Dalit schoolgirl arrived at school and walked into her classroom, where the schoolteacher was a Brahmin. At break time, the young schoolgirl walked over to the water tank, as she was thirsty, but when she touched the communal water cup and went to take a drink of water, the schoolteacher snapped. He beat the young schoolgirl so mercilessly that he actually dislodged one of her eyeballs from the socket. Dalits had to be shown their proper place, by any means necessary, as it were, including a disgraceful amount of violence by those who have privilege against those who clearly don't.

So, what are we to do with this schoolteacher, a person with Brahmin privilege who has engaged in an overt act of violent discrimination? The answer is easy. Put him on the next Air India flight to San Francisco, because as soon as he arrives and walks into the airport, he becomes a person of color incapable of privilege and oppression. The social construct must hold, so we launder his privilege for him. Now he can only be a victim, never an oppressor.

In short, the social construct of white privilege holds, but at what cost? What do we say to the young Dalit schoolgirl, or to the many Afro-Colombians who face racism every day of their lives? What we say to them is nothing. We can offer only silence. Their suffering must be occluded and erased, written off as an inconvenience that gets in the way of those who need to believe that white privilege is real. A social construct that is meant to highlight oppression ends up concealing it instead.

Lastly, please take note that with the new definition of racism I have offered in this book, the very concept of white privilege is itself racist. It excludes by race, singling out whites from all others, and it encourages others to think negatively about whites. But in our current state of diversity, the social construct of white privilege is clung to like an ideological life raft on a raging social sea, because it allows ideas such as the inability of people of color to be racist to persist. It's how we end up with shows with titles like *Dear White People*, which emphasize that only one group is the problem, that only whites are responsible for all our social ills. If we are truly serious about confronting racism, what we need instead is a show called *Dear People*. To sweep aside the suffering of the Dalit schoolgirl or the Afro-Colombian or the millions of others whose pain must be denied simply to uphold the social construct of white privilege is an unacceptably high price to pay. Racism and privilege are everywhere and they don't just come in one color. To see it any other way is not just to tolerate injustice—it is to be complicit in it.

CHAPTER 4

TESTING DIVERSITY

Where to begin in the process of fixing diversity? One place to start, and this is the focus of this chapter, is to create a series of tests that can help us determine whether any particular action or gesture or policy is going to help us move toward the kind of mutual understanding we need in order to cultivate a new diversity that will work well and work for all of us. These aren't the kinds of tests that one studies for, but rather they are tests in the sense that one might test the limits of something or test for the presence of intelligent life on Mars or in Miami. In other words, they are tests that will help us map out a new set of collective parameters for how we engage in diversity and how we situate ourselves among others. As I hope I have made clear by now, diversity is a civic responsibility that we all bear equally, so these tests are meant to apply equally to all of us. A new diversity requires a new demeanor, a new attitude, a new outlook, and a new set of principles. This chapter is the workshop where we start to build a new diversity, the forge where we meld the old into the new, the kiln where we take the half-baked diversity we now have and fully bake it into something durable and beautiful. It's time to roll up our sleeves and get busy with the work that needs to be done.

Testing Diversity: How to tell right from wrong
One of the most common things often said when it comes to determining whether something like hate speech or racism or prejudice has occurred is that it somehow "depends on the context." This argument is frequently offered as a default answer to the complex questions generated by the fact that identity is rarely a simple matter. This is why I spent so much time talking about *posturing* in a previous chapter—it short circuits the need to find answers to complex questions by making identity into an act where all we need to do is *go* through the motions rather than *think* through the motions. It seems to me that if we are going to try to make better sense of the complexities of identity, in a way that allows us to develop a true sense of mutual understanding that, as I have argued repeatedly, is the one thing that diversity ought to be based on, then we need something more than the idea that every single question of identity has to be answered by the specific details of the context within which it occurred. It seems to me that we need at least some general rules to get out of the every-instance-is-unique mindset that makes general understanding impossible.

I won't say that all of the rules I will offer here are foolproof—no set of rules ever is. Consider them proposals, rather than hard-and-fast, inflexible regulations. But I at least hope this will get us started on a new sort of dialogue, a new way of talking about things to move on and move ahead of the stale discussions we have now, if we have any discussion at all. We need to talk about identity and we need to talk about how to situate and understand ourselves among others. I sometimes think we compartmentalize all of our thoughts on identity and diversity into three neatly separated and mutually exclusive files: Lies We Tell Ourselves about Ourselves, Lies We Tell Ourselves about Others, and Lies We Tell Others about Ourselves. Hopefully a set of tests, a set of mutually–agreed upon guidelines, can help us build a new and better filing system than that. So without further delay, I now present a handy fits-in-your-pocket and please-do-try-this-at-home-and-everywhere-else set of tests to push our endless discussions on diversity in a new and constructive direction. This is where we craft a new diversity for a new America.

Test #1: The Private-Public Test
The private public test states that *a diversity-related policy or practice is universally and equitably desirable if you would want that policy or practice to be implemented in your private life to the same degree as it is in public life.* In some ways it is a safeguard against NIMBYism (Not In My Back Yard-ism), which is the tendency many persons have of advocating things as long somebody else has to deal with the consequences. Many people, for instance, advocate building more prisons so that more people can be put behind bars, but balk at the idea of having any of those prisons built in or near their own neighborhoods. In Berkeley, many people advocate that the homeless population, which in Berkeley is quite large, be allowed free access to urban space and call on Berkeleyans to treat the homeless with compassion and dignity, but those same advocates tend to be the first to call the police when the homeless show up in their own neighborhoods.

In an earlier chapter I pointed out how most advocates of what is called "immigration reform" come from Latino and Hispanic communities largely because the vast majority of undocumented immigrants, known also as illegal immigrants to some, come from those communities. In terms of diversity and demographics, immigration reform is a huge boost to the demographic numbers of those communities, which makes it a thinly-disguised form of community activism that advocates granting citizenship and amnesty in order to expand the numbers in those communities. Alongside this there is also a call to change the very language that we use to discuss immigration reform. The term "illegal alien" or "illegal immigrant" is considered offensive and discriminatory, the advocates of immigration reform claim, because it implies that the person is inherently illegal (as opposed to the act itself). Attend any rally on immigration reform and you will find at least one person carrying a sign that reads "No person is illegal," and sometimes, "Immigration is a human right."

As for the latter claim, this is a sad case of what I would call badly misinformed activism. Immigration is actually not a human right at all. Indeed, the Migrant Workers Convention (1990), which is probably the most important international human rights document we have that protects the rights of workers who cross borders, states very clearly that no one has an inherent right to immigrate to another country for work, and that only migrant workers who migrate legally and abide by all of the laws of the host country are protected by the rights listed in the document. Indeed, there is nothing in *any* human rights document that requires a country to offer amnesty or accept a foreign citizen that they do not want to accept.

While I am on the topic, I may as well take a moment to address the issue of using the term "illegal immigrant" versus "undocumented immigrant," and also some of the legal confusion surrounding the whole idea of immigration. I feel it necessary to do so because it is a poisonously and acrimoniously contentious debate, one that came up over and over again in the 2016 presidential election campaigns and no doubt will continue to do so for some time to come. The charge from those who support the use of "undocumented immigrant" or "undocumented resident" is that the use of the term "illegal immigrant" is not only incorrect, because no person is illegal, but also it is an intentional act of discrimination or racism, since it is directed primarily at persons of Latino heritage.

Let's start with the first point, that the use of the phrase "illegal immigrant" is incorrect. I'm not advocating for its use, but we should at least open up a discussion about it. We frequently associate a person with the act they commit, especially when the act is a criminal act. If a person commits rape, for instance, we call that person a rapist. If a person commits murder, we call them a murderer. If a person breaks into a house and steals money, we call that person a thief. If a person enters a house without permission and stays there as a squatter, we can call that person an illegal occupant of the house. We name the person for the illegal act they committed, and we do it all the time. I don't think anyone would think of it as discriminatory if I called someone a thief, on the grounds that the person only committed one act of theft (stealing my wallet) but at all other times in their life was not stealing something. Nor would anyone be enamored with the idea of using euphemisms so as not to hurt the feelings of persons who committed illegal acts. "He's not a thief, he's the undocumented owner of possessions that are legally mine." So the thing is, if a person immigrates to a country illegally, that person could rightfully be called an illegal immigrant. The difference between a "person who immigrated illegally" and an "illegal immigrant" is one of semantics. Since usage of the phrase "illegal immigrant" follows the same linguistic patterns as for other illegal acts, it cannot be seen as inherently discriminatory. And no, I am not equating illegal immigration with rape and murder, but what all of those labels have in common is that they refer to people who have committed illegal acts.

This leads me to the other part of the opposition to the phrase "illegal immigrant," which is either that immigration is not a crime, or that the phrase describes the person as inherently illegal, giving rise to the slogan, "no person is illegal." I've already covered the semantic part of this—crossing an international border without permission is illegal anywhere in the world, and entering a country that is not one's own is immigration, so illegal immigration is technically correct. But the other part of "no human is illegal" rests upon the argument that immigration is a human right, that any person has a right to seek a better life elsewhere for themselves or for their family. That's a very nice way of thinking, but it has no rooting in reality. International law is very clear that the border of a country is like the door of your house—no one can enter without legal permission, otherwise it's an illegal act. There is no right to enter another country just because it's nicer than the one you're in, just as there is no right to start living in someone else's house just because it's nicer than yours. Undocumented immigrants in the US are entitled to due process as much as anyone else—those who argue that since they are here illegally they have no rights are dead wrong about that—but America is exceptional in that regard, and the due process rights that undocumented residents can claim are constitutional rights, not human rights. As bad as things are, America is far more compassionate and generous in the rights it offers to undocumented immigrants than nearly every other country in the world.

But back to the Private-Public test. Here is one example of how it works. Since I was talking about immigration reform, let's take that as a public law for starters. Advocates of immigration reform argue that anyone should be allowed to come into the country, whether through legal or illegal means (open borders), and that once inside, the United States should allow them to stay and should stop trying to arrest or deport such persons. In the interest of diversity and humanity, the citizens of the United States should pay to support all such people and for all such services that facilitate their relocation to America. Anything else is considered discrimination. That's the public part.

Now let's look at the private equivalent of this. The "open border" policy advocated for the country would translate into an "unlocked door" policy for the home. Indeed, the very idea of a lock on the door at all, much like the idea of a wall at the border, would be inherently offensive and discriminatory—as if it would be acceptable that we should let only some people into our homes but not others. And it wouldn't just be as a shelter for the homeless. It would be for anyone who wanted a better life. If you have a three bedroom house and a family with a one-bedroom house walks by and thinks your place would offer a better life, then they have absolutely every right to walk in (because the door should be open to all) and start living there—and living there would include utilizing all of the services that you pay for. I could go on, but for now, I am sure you get the idea.

If you are like pretty much anyone I know, if you came home and discovered that someone had entered your home illegally—without documents (which you as a house owner have)—the first thing you would do is call 911 and report that there is an intruder in your house. (And imagine if the police tell you in response that it's wrong to use the word "intruder" and they scold you for being so offensive. You should use the term "unauthorized guest" instead.) I can't think of a single person who wouldn't do that, and for me, what that means is that immigration reform fails the Private-Public Test. We are advocating things in public life that we would not tolerate or want in private life. The questions we should ask of diversity policy and practice are not "is this good for me?" or "is this good for my community?" but rather "is this good for everyone?" or "is this thing I am advocating a universally good thing?" And if in answering these questions, we apply Private-Public Test and the answer fails the test, then we should not be advocating that policy or practice for diversity.

I know there are also those who will claim that America was founded on the idea of immigration, that we are all immigrants and it is hypocritical if not downright un-American to restrict immigration now. So yes, in America in 1776, we had open borders. But we also had slavery, and laws that said women couldn't vote, and we certainly didn't have marriage equality. What happened? Things changed. We are no longer the nation we were in 1776, and that is as true for the social values we hold as it is for the world we live in. It's foolish to think that we should hold onto an immigration ideal we had over 200 years ago. That doesn't mean we should build a wall (which I think is a foolish idea), but it does mean that rethinking immigration is not necessarily a discriminatory or racist thing.

The Private-Public Test is therefore one test to help demonstrate the inconsistencies in the advocacy of policies and practices that relate to diversity (and immigration reform is often discussed in the context of "diversifying America"). It is not, however, the only test to use as a general guide, because not every situation is amenable to the Public-Private comparison. For other situations, we will need something more.

Test #2: The Water Fountain Test
The Water Fountain Test takes its name for the sad and lamentable and quite frankly outrageous chapter in American history in which we had separate water fountains for use by different racial groups—one for whites, and another (usually dirtier and inferior) for pretty much everyone else, but mostly for blacks. It was part of the whole "separate but equal" mentality that was legally swept away in *Brown v. Board of Education* (1954), which ruled that separate but equal (and they were hardly equal) school systems were unconstitutional. The legal grounds were set to bring an end once and for all to the practice of segregation, not just in education but in every sector of public life. So based on that, the Water Fountain Test states that *anything that is reserved for one identity group alone and is not equally available to or accessible for all other groups should not be tolerated and should be dismantled in order for diversity to work properly.*

I used immigration reform as an example of the first test, so for this test I will also use an illustrative example, in this case, hate speech. In fact, I will just jump right in and go for glory by using the most divisive and polarizing word we probably have in the English language: the N-word. Now, unless you have been living most of your life with one or more fingers stuck in a light-socket, you probably have had a moment to reflect on and realize just how offensive and racially-charged this word is. You might also be puzzled by the fact that in spite of this, the word remains in circulation—for many Americans, not a day goes by without hearing that word at least once. You would think that in an era of diversity, at a time when more and more people are concerned about the prevalence of racism, that such an offensive word would be on the way out, on the fast track to lexical extinction.

So how is it that we still have this word in circulation? The simplistic answer would be that we still have it around because there is still so much white racism and because white people like to use this word to disparage and oppress black people. That might have once been true, but now no longer is. Now we have a different sort of issue with this word, which is the existence of differential standards of usage among identity-based groups. In short, only some identity groups can use this word, while others cannot.

Before I go any further, let me just say with absolute clarity that I am NOT advocating that we should all be able to use the N-word. I am saying the opposite. I am saying that any word that is only available to one group but not others is probably not a word we should have in circulation at all.

In more specific terms, the N-word has been taken over, "appropriated" to use a fancier word, in order to take its power away from the original user, white people, and to hand that power over to the original victim of the racist word, black people. The idea is that if the black community takes the word and puts it into wide circulation among their own community, then it would divest the word of its discriminatory power and divest the white community of the power it held over the black community through the deployment of that word. With the rise of civil rights law and the rise of specific laws and standards regarding hate-speech, we now have a situation where any usage of that word can be considered an offensive act of racism—*unless* it is uttered by a black person.

And yes, I have heard various justifications for this exceptional allowance, for instance that the use of N-word in the black community is a community-affirming word that collectively commemorates the survival of a shared historical experience of oppression, and so on. Yet there are many African-Americans who use the word to refer disparagingly to certain sub-sections of the black community, and of course its usage in rap lyrics and in hip-hop culture has become ubiquitous, sometimes with negative meanings and sometimes with what are seen as empowering meanings. There are yet others who want to separate the N-word from its differently-spelled variants, such as the N-word spelled with an –a at the end rather than an –er (often with a plural ending in –az), but I don't think this holds up well under even minimal scrutiny. If slightly changing the spelling of offensive words makes them acceptable, or at least no longer problematic, then be prepared for whole new onslaught of hate speech from all directions, all of it slightly misspelled and therefore beyond the realm of standards of offensiveness, civil rights, racism, and so forth. Imagine a defendant explaining to a judge in a case over the use of homophobic hate-speech: "Your Honor, when I called this person a fag, in my head I was thinking of faeg or fayag, and so the different spelling takes away all of the offensiveness and completely changes everything." Seriously, just try to make the argument in any court of law, or anywhere for that matter. Then sit back and listen to the endless sound of guffaws, chuckles, and chortles. And when the verdict comes in, no doubt the judge would be the first to declare that you've been convicted of premeditated idiocy (and oh, do I so wish that were really a crime).

The Water Fountain Test gives us one way of cutting through all these different contexts and different intentions of usage. It simply asks: Is it right for one community to have something—the right to use a word, for instance—that is denied to every other community? We wouldn't and shouldn't accept it with water fountains or schools, so why do we accept it with words? Even if the usage of the N-word did at some point represent a collective act of appropriation and resistance against a derogatory word that symbolized unequal power relations between whites and blacks, that purpose no longer really applies, and more than anything what this word does now is draw a divide between one community and everyone else. It entrenches the enclave mentality (discussed earlier) and makes meaningful diversity more difficult by undermining our equal access to a common language.

I am not saying we should all want equal access to that word, and I am not sure the Lenny Bruce approach, where we all use it as much as possible to render it completely harmless, is what we need right now either. But there is something troubling about creating the precedent that only people of a certain identity can use a particular word, and can even use it to refer offensively to others in the same community, while others cannot. The Water Fountain Test says that either we can all use it, or none of us can. If you can imagine a water fountain that spews our words rather than water, I would not want to walk into a building and see a sign that says "blacks only," any more than I would want to see one that said "whites only, or "Latinos only," or "Muslims only," and so forth.

The differential use rights also play out in differential judgments over the use of the word. Many a black comedian uses the word in their performance, yet very few others from different identity-groups dare to use the word. I already mentioned in an earlier chapter the N-word-filled rant of comedian Michael Richards, a rant that pretty much derailed his entire career and spawned endless apologies. More recently, celebrity chef Paula Deen, best known for artery-clogging recipes and a lard-should-be-a-food-group approach to cooking, watched her entire career and business empire nearly collapse when news broke that she had used the N-word. I'm not saying there should be no consequences about the use of the N-word, just pointing how the differential use rights create grotesquely uneven expectations about who can use the word, when they can, why (if ever) they can, and how they can. Many an advocate for legal reform in the United States has pointed out the injustice that offenders are often given differentially severe punishments depending on their racial or ethnic identity, so it seems to me equally unjust to do the same with hate words and hate speech. No separate or differential punishments—period.

There is also the sad reality that we have lots of words in circulation that are ethnic, racial, religious, or sexist slurs, and we have no uniform or consistent way to compare them for the harm they create or the offense they generate. The word "cracker" for instance—witness Rachel Jeantel using the word to refer to George Zimmerman in the trial over the shooting of Trayvon Martin—is clearly a racially-charged word used to insult white people. In that sense it is closely-related to the word "honky"—think of the line from the popular Macklemore song "Thrift Shop" that goes "Damn, that's a cold-ass honky"—which in its etymological origins emerged as a pejorative and racially-charged term that blacks could use against whites.

Yet if the notions of hate-speech and racism are brought up, invariably and rapidly someone will point out that "cracker" and "honky" are not as bad as the N-word, and "nowhere near" as offensive. But is that really an issue? Can we really measure and compare the inherent offensiveness of words such as these? Words aren't like chili peppers, which are ranked on a heat-scale according to the number of Scoville units they contain. We have no way of testing which words are "too bad" to use or which words are worse than others, and we need a better rule or test than merely leaving every instance of the use of these words to context and interpretation. If diversity is about equality then I don't see how we can reconcile that with completely differential standards regarding the very words that are used to describe our identities, positively or negatively. The Water Fountain Test at least tries to put us all on the same standard, and I really don't see how it could be a problem to use the Water Fountain Test to try to take all pejorative and racist and hate-filled speech out of circulation once and for all. If the N-word were laid to rest forever, I don't think any of us should miss it.

Test #3: The Reciprocity Test
The Reciprocity Tests requires that *whatever you demand for yourself from others you should also offer to others on your own*. I suppose it is something like a diversity variant of the Golden Rule (do for others as you would have them do for you), but it is nevertheless an important test to consider when working out a new type of diversity that is equitable and inclusive for all. The test can be applied geographically, culturally, or conceptually, at the very least, and can probably be applied in many other ways as well. For this test, I am going to look at the very controversial aspect of ethnic-based neighborhoods and the debate over inclusion and exclusion in the demarcation of residential terrain. I think most people, and hopefully all people, would accept the premise that excluding people from living in a neighborhood or from renting an apartment simply on account of their identity—race, ethnicity, religion, sexual orientation, what have you—is an act of discrimination, plain and simple. There has been a long litany of lawsuits and court rulings and housing policies that are designed to ensure our civil right to live in a place of our own choosing, and to make that choice without fear of discrimination or prejudice. The old and oft-heard phrase of "there goes the neighborhood," originally meant to invoke the reluctant sigh and plaint of the white man in his white neighborhood as one by one, non-white families exercised their civil rights and moved into the neighborhood to settle, should be a thing of the past. And of course there are still those who still wish things would just go back to the way they were, where different groups lived in different spaces and led separate lives, but that too needs to remain a thing of the past.

At this point, however, I need to introduce a word that is probably familiar to everyone, but needs to be discussed in the context of the Reciprocity Test. That word is *gentrification*. Gentrification refers to the process of in-migration to urban areas, usually poorer urban areas with a high percentage of residents from non-dominant communities, by higher-income persons whose expanded presence in the area drives up property values and also (the argument goes) the general cost of living. The higher property values create higher taxes, and that, coupled with higher costs of general living, tends to displace many of the former inhabitants from the neighborhood, thereby changing the identity-group demographics, sometimes significantly and almost always irrevocably. What I have always found strange and a little unsettling about discussions of gentrification is that the very same people who denounce any attempt, real or imagined, by white residents in white (or mostly white) neighborhoods to keep non-white minorities from moving in to settle, at the same time champion the exclusion of whites (and others) from non-white neighborhoods on the grounds that the dominant non-white communities in those neighborhoods have to preserve their "cultural environment." In Berkeley, I have even heard people—self-styled "community activists"—refer to the process of gentrification as "cultural genocide" (which is legally incorrect on multiple levels, but in Berkeley, being incorrect has never been seen as an obstacle to activism).

If we apply the Reciprocity Test, we can immediately see the problem. We cannot have an approach to diversity that says, in short: "You have to open up your neighborhood to me, but I can shut mine to you." That fails the Reciprocity Test, clearly and simply. The phrase "there goes the neighborhood"—which as I have said is associated with a sort of white man's lachrymose dirge to the passing of his neighborhood from white to non-white—is based on the twin problems of (1) the loss of the cultural character of the neighborhood ("white" in this case being a culture) and (2) the feared shift in property values, usually in a downward direction, that will occur as the neighborhood changes. Both of these are also in play when it comes to gentrification.

Opponents of gentrification often complain that it will change the cultural character of the neighborhood: a black neighborhood should remain black, for instance, or a Latino one should remain Latino. But the Reciprocity Test states that there is no more reason for a black neighborhood to remain black as there is for a white neighborhood to remain white. If it is good to diversify a white neighborhood, then it is good to diversify a black neighborhood. In both cases the enclave is eroded, which as I argued earlier, is a good thing for diversity. And as for property values, whether the shift is upward or downward, this is not a sufficient or even acceptable reason to prevent new people from settling into a neighborhood. Diversity—meaningful diversity, that is—requires sacrifices from all groups and not just some, and no diversity worth working for is going to come on the cheap. Diversity has costs associated with it, and those costs need to be borne by all groups—it is part of the civic responsibility of diversity that I discussed earlier. Indeed, if we don't bear the costs equally—if our approach is "diversity is expensive so how about if you pay for it while I am exempt"—that also fails the Reciprocity Test.

As a reminder, when the US Supreme Court endorsed diversity as an inherent social good in the *Grutter* (2003) decision, they did not only endorse it for white dominant areas. They endorsed it for *all* areas. In the San Francisco Bay Area, however, when people hear, for example, that Marin County is 72% white, the response is usually that Marin County "lacks diversity" and therefore needs more of it (people of color should move in). Yet if there is a neighborhood that is 98% Latino, for instance, it is referred to as a "diverse community," even though it lacks any discernible diversity. We use a differential standard that fails the Reciprocity Test—people of color should move to Marin County to "add diversity," but a predominantly Latino neighborhood is already inherently diverse so having others move in (gentrification) means the neighborhood would "lose diversity."

To see how all of this comes together in action we can take a look at the Boyle Heights neighborhood in Los Angeles. Boyle Heights is a traditionally Latino neighborhood that has seen an influx of non-Latinos in recent years, many of whom have been "rent refugees" (California term) who cannot afford to live in the city center and so move to neighborhoods where the cost of living is cheaper. As is supposed to happen with diversity, they also bring an influx of new ideas and new cultural patterns, yet, as I just mentioned, this is interpreted by residents in these neighborhoods not as gaining diversity, but as losing diversity. In November 2016, residents of Boyle Heights woke up to find anti-white graffiti spray-painted on various art galleries and other cultural points in the neighborhood. "Fu_k white art!" is just one example of the message that was sent (slightly edited by me, but let's just say the word isn't "funk"). Yet when police decided to investigate this as a possible hate crime—keeping in mind here the persistent belief that people of color cannot be racist and thus can never commit hate crimes—community activists became enraged. "You're talking about spray-painting a wall with truth," said one, adding, "Whoever wrote that is hurting and is angry." Apparently, racism isn't racism if you are angry.[13] Another activist referred to the graffiti as "righteous anger," something to be celebrated. If you thought I was overstating the case in an earlier chapter when I talked about how colonialism and imperialism are always assumed to be white and always seen as the moment

---

13 Rory Carroll, "'Anti-white' graffiti in gentrifying LA neighborhood sparks hate crime debate," *The Guardian* (November 4, 2016) at https://www.theguardian.com/us-news/2016/nov/04/boyle-heights-art-gallery-vandalism-hate-crime-gentrification

when the world went wrong, then consider this quote from another community activist in Boyle Heights: "We're the colonized resisting colonization." Even the president of the neighborhood council linked the art galleries to "a certain level of privilege," which, if you're not seeing it yet, refers to white privilege. You can see how this all fails the Reciprocity Test. You should also see how it is a flagrant display of everything that has gone wrong with diversity in America.

The same rule applies to things beyond our neighborhoods. I teach at a university and one of the things I hear pretty much every day is that UC Berkeley "needs more diversity." As I think I have made clear throughout this book, the majority of people who promote diversity have no idea what they are actually talking about, but even if I just accept this statement at full value, that diversity makes for a better environment in which to learn, then the Reciprocity Test tells me that if it is good at my university then it must also be good at yours. So what do we do if your university is a place like Howard University, one of many "historically black" universities in America?

The good news is that in recent years many historically black college campuses have started to accept more students from other identity-groups, including whites, but still, the percentage of black students enrolled in these campuses remains an overwhelming majority, some as high as 95%, and there is ongoing debate as to whether black colleges should be exempt from diversity requirements. Similar to debates on gentrification, the idea is that black colleges should be allowed to avoid diversity so they can preserve the cultural environment of their campuses. According to one student at Howard University: "Although I appreciate all races and have friends of all kinds back home, I definitely think that Howard was created for black students and the integrity of the majority black institution should remain that way...I don't see why other races would attend when it was created for the benefit and growth of our black race and culture."[14] That of course is the opinion of just one student and as I have pointed out, this is part of an ongoing debate, which means that there are others who favor expanding the enrollment of non-black students at historically black colleges. But I think the Reciprocity Test can play a useful role in pushing these and other debates forward, and can help to root out so much of the hypocrisy that poisons so much of diversity as we currently have it. We can't move forward weighed down by the burden of so much hypocrisy. Whether it is a neighborhood or a college campus, we should not be championing homogeneous enclaves, nor should we be asking others to make sacrifices and implement change while we stand back and consider ourselves exempt.

Think, too, of the company one keeps in opposing something like gentrification. Anti-gentrification activists—and again, we really should refer to them as anti-diversification activists—argue among other things that gentrification (diversification) is wrong because a black neighborhood should remain black, or a Latino neighborhood should remain Latino, or an Asian neighborhood (or a Chinatown) should remain Asian, and so forth. But the same activists do not hesitate to lambast movements to limit immigration or diversity in places like France, Germany, or even the US, when those movements advocate that Germany should remain German, or France should remain French, and so forth. Anti-gentrification activists have no problem labeling those movements as alt-right, fascist, neo-Nazi, racist, and any one of a number of other negative labels. Opposing immigration into a country is alt-right hate, but opposing immigration into a neighborhood is "progressive activism"? No, the two sentiments—anti-gentrification

---

14 Alyssa Paddock, "Historically black colleges are seeing an increase in white students," *The Washington Post* (May 17, 2013) at http://www.washingtonpost.com/blogs/therootdc/post/historically-black-colleges-are-seeing-an-increase-of-white-students/2013/05/17/5a642f5e-bd80-11e2-89c9-3be8095fe767_blog.html

and anti-immigration—are exactly the same, and thus this fails the Reciprocity Test. If "no person is illegal," then a person has just as much of a right to enter a country as they do to enter a neighborhood. Critics of the anti-immigration movements in places like Germany, France, or elsewhere laugh at the claim of "preserving German culture" (for instance) because, they claim, one cannot define German culture or German cultural values, so there is nothing to preserve. Yet it is as difficult to define German culture as it is to define black culture (for instance), so there is no substance to the claim of preserving black culture by keeping a neighborhood black (or Latino, etc.). If you want all to be welcome at the border of the country, then the Reciprocity Test requires you to want all to be welcome at the border of the neighborhood, too.

Test #4: The Consistency Test
The consistency test asks that in any situation where diversity is a central concern, *what we ask for in one situation should be the same that we ask for in any other similar situation.* Again, it's a stand against hypocrisy, this time from yet another different angle. What it means is that if you want somebody to understand you, or if you are frustrated that they don't understand you to the level you want, then you need to make the same effort to understand them right back. We need consistency not just in terms of behavior but also in terms of ethics and responsibility. If you think America is stupid because it doesn't understand your religion, ask yourself how many other religions *you* know well. That's the general idea.

Let's take, for example, the oft-heard exhortation that Americans should learn more about Islam—an exhortation, by the way, that I fully endorse. The idea is that most of the anti-Muslim bigotry and discrimination in America originates, like most bigotry and discrimination does, out of ignorance. If we can fix ignorance, we can fix bigotry and end discrimination. So far, so good. But if the expectation is that non-Muslims need to do more to learn about Islam, then it must also be the case, according to the Consistency Test, that Muslims need to do more to learn about non-Muslim religions. If you are going to ask a Christian to study and learn more about Islam, then you should equally expect a Muslim to study and learn more about, say, Hinduism. And if you're thinking that isn't right because there is only the issue of bigotry and discrimination *against* Muslims by non-Muslims, and no bigotry and discrimination *by* Muslims against non-Muslims, then you need to study and learn more about a lot of things.

To push the point a bit further, I could even point out that our entire conversation on diversity pretty much fails the Consistency Test. When, for instance, was the last time you read an article about Islamic homophobia? I'm not talking about hate-filled blogs or the extremist press on the left or the right. I'm talking about your basic mainstream media in America. You're probably struggling to remember an article on that topic, and the reason is simple. To write about Islamic homophobia might make Islam look bad, and therefore it might be considered Islamophobic to write about it. Even in the aftermath of horrible events such as the Orlando shooting of June 12, 2016, in which Omar Mateen killed 49 people and wounded 58 more at a gay nightclub, commentators stumbled over their words. To point out that Omar Mateen was a Muslim might be seen as Islamophobic, so for some at least, it was easier to blame conservative Christians for creating a homophobic "environment of hate" in America that either directly or indirectly caused the Orlando massacre. I agree there is a good deal of homophobic rhetoric emanating from the Christian right, but what I am getting at here is the way our discussion of anything relating to diversity fails the Consistency Test. We need to be consistent in our discourse, which means we should be able to talk as openly about Islamic homophobia as we do about Christian homophobia, or any religious-based homophobia for that matter.

The point is, we need to remember that diversity, at least a diversity that is worth having (and the one I've been talking about all along), is a project of *mutual* understanding. Anyone can assemble a group of different people together in a room and have them just stand there, side by side, looking a little awkward perhaps, but otherwise just displaying their difference like a bunch of token crayons in a human-sized crayon box. But for diversity to happen, for a meaningful and vibrant and constructive diversity to happen, each person in the room has to make an equal and equally consistent effort to understand everyone else in the room. And if that is the way it works in that room, then it should be the way it works in all other situations—in the classroom, in the office, at the park, on the plane—wherever you find yourself. If you want it here, then give it there and give it everywhere. I don't think there is a judicial or legal system anywhere in the world that does not require consistency to ensure that justice prevails. Diversity, being a form of social justice, should require nothing less.

Test #5: The General-Specific Test
The General-Specific Test asks that *we refrain from making judgments or statements that attribute general characteristics to an identity-based group based on specific events or occurrences.* This is something of an "anti-profiling" test, but since profiling has come to take on both very specific and impossibly vague meanings, this test is something different from just a general warning against profiling. Some of this is quite easy to spot and defuse: when one African-American commits a crime, we cannot conclude that all blacks are criminals, or when one Muslim extremist carries out a terrorist attack, we cannot conclude that all Muslims are terrorists. But we have to apply these tests equally across the board, and apply them to each identity group to ensure fairness and to ensure that we get a diversity that works equally well for all of us. So, for instance, just as we cannot conclude that all blacks are criminals because

of the criminal actions of a few individuals, we cannot conclude, à la Charlottesville, that all whites are racist because of the racist actions of some white people.

I hear over and over again, at least in my professional experience, that whites are racists and that white racism is institutionalized. Yet if I press that issue and ask for specifics, what I hear are random examples that deal with specific instances. To make such a blanket statement is itself a racist generalization generated by specific acts or occurrences—meaning it fails the General-Specific Test (and is thus an invalid statement). Even for something as widespread as slavery, it would still be incorrect to make the statement, "whites are responsible for slavery." *Some* whites are certainly responsible for slavery, but not all whites (and as we saw earlier, non-white populations also participated in the American slave trade). Generalized statements about specific acts or occurrences are poisonous to the work of diversity, and so no matter how difficult it is, we need to apply the General-Specific Test and make better assessments of each other in looking at the problems of society.

Here is a more specific example of how this works. In February 2012, an article appeared on ESPN's website about New York Knicks' basketball star Jeremy Lin that used the phrase "chink in the armor." The word "chink" of course is a racial slur against people of Asian heritage, which would include Jeremy Lin, but the phrase "chink in the armor" is also a legitimate phrase in the English language that in any other context would have no racial meaning whatsoever. Nevertheless, the outcry was quick and fierce, and even though the ESPN sports writer who wrote the headline stated that he was mortified by the mistake and hadn't even thought of the link between the racial slur and the English phrase, ESPN ended up firing him. The blogospheres lit-up and op-eds were churned out to point out how this one event showed the reality of white racism in America. Yet, if we apply the General-Specific Test, we can see the problem here. All we can say about this incident at best is that one sports writer and one editor made a mistake (and if the sports writer is correct, an unintentional one at that). We cannot make a leap to the general claim that because one writer used the word "chink," all whites are complicit in the act. It is no more legitimate to do that than it is to read a headline about a robbery carried out by an African-American man and conclude that African-American men must therefore all be thieves, or to argue, as many do, that one Muslim carrying out a terrorist attack is evidence that all Muslims are terrorists. All of those statements fail the General-Specific Test.

(On a side note, though clearly the word "chink" is a racial slur when used as such, there have been a surprisingly large number of similar cases and complaints regarding the use of the word "niggardly," even though the word has no historical or etymological connection whatsoever to the N-word.)

Even when it comes to more extreme events, the General-Specific Test can help keep the dialogue open, especially in moments when we desperately need that to happen. We can look here, for instance, to the events that transpired in Ferguson, a suburb of St. Louis, Missouri, in August 2014. On Saturday, August 9, police officer Darren Wilson, who was white, had an "encounter" (I'm using the most neutral term I can) with Michael Brown, who was black, which ended with the shooting death of Michael Brown by Darren Wilson. Though calls for justice quickly emerged, the specific events of the encounter, which involved one white police officer and one black civilian, quickly transformed into a larger and more general claim of "white racism" against "victimized blacks." This is where the General-Specific Test can help, by keeping us focused on the specifics, such as whether or not Darren Wilson's actions were legally justified and whether or not he followed proper police procedure. Even if we could prove that Darren Wilson was a racist or that his actions were racially motivated, that would only tell us something about Darren Wilson. It doesn't tell us something about all white people. I want justice, too, but we will get better justice for all by keeping a sense of perspective, as difficult as that can be in the midst of tragic events. Generalizations rarely bring us closer to justice.

The General-Specific Test is designed to keep us from making generalizations that we should not be making and generalizations that lead us into the type of prejudice and discrimination that are so anathema to the principles of a truly vibrant system of diversity. We cannot extrapolate from the specific acts of the few to the general characterizations of the many. It doesn't even have to be "the few" that we reference. Sometimes a single act by a single individual is then extrapolated to the whole group. The hate-filled generalizations that so many people harbor have no place in a diverse America—"all Muslims are terrorists," or "all blacks are criminals," or "all whites are racists"—all of these fail the General-Specific Test and all of them need to be broken down and dismantled and discarded in order for the prejudice to end and the healing to begin. And with that healing comes understanding, and only with that understanding comes the diversity we need and the diversity we deserve.

Test #6: The Past and Present Test
The last test for diversity that I will offer is the Past and Present Test, *which states that we have to refrain from making judgments and accusations in the present based upon the actions of the past.* There is a reason I spent so much time talking about history in earlier discussions, because history plays such a prominent role not only in the articulation of identity in the present but also in the articulation of historical grievances of the past that some believe need to be settled in the present. This is generally a fallacious idea, in terms of history, logic, and law. In American law, for instance, and quite frankly in any legal system that has even a remote claim to fairness and consistency, one cannot hold a person accountable

in the present for a crime committed by someone else, even a close relative, in the past. The police cannot come to your door and say, "We just discovered that your grandfather robbed a bank and was never caught, but since he is dead, you will have to go to jail instead." Only the person who committed the actual crime can be held accountable, and we cannot historically generalize or historically attribute guilt and blame across chronological divides. It is tough to let the past be the past, so if we treat diversity as some kind of instrument to change and "correct" the past, we are in essence trying to hold people in the present accountable for the crimes of the past, crimes they never committed or had any control over.

One of the strange peculiarities of diversity discourse, at least as we currently have it, is the strong attraction that many identity-groups have to the idea of victimization. In most cases, that victimization impulse stems from a link of the past to the present, and the sense of victimization lingers in the present, awaiting a resolution that for the most part can never happen. Many people, and to a certain extent even the entire judicial system before the *Grutter* decision of the Supreme Court, looked at diversity as a sort of settlement for all historical injustices, and that list of injustices kept getting longer and longer. Being a victim was an attractive facet of identity to claim because it made it clear that one was "innocent" of historical crimes and as a matter of current policy could be on the receiving (benefitting) end of whatever benefits diversity could provide rather than on the giving (sacrificing) end. But going back to the principle of the law I just cited, it is as unfair as it is illegal (though it would never go to trial) to force a person to make a sacrifice in the present for an action committed by another person in the past. This is why the Supreme Court quite rightly stepped away from this principle in the *Grutter* decision and refocused diversity on how we interact in the present rather than accounting for what others did in the past.

Unpoisoning the Well

I know there are people who fervently believe that anyone who benefitted from the systems set up by the evil-doers of the past, including people who benefit in the present, are equally culpable and complicit in those crimes so it is considered acceptable to have them pay or make sacrifices in the present for what was done in the past. But think, for instance, of the unexpected example of Yale University. Many a person has attended and graduated from Yale, and no doubt many a person has gone on to do wonderful things with their education. But Yale University was founded in 1701 by Elihu Yale, and Elihu Yale, before he founded what became Yale University, was a governor of the British East India Company in Madras (now Chennai), India. Yep, for those of you who think (European) imperialism and colonialism were the worst things to happen in human history (see earlier chapters to see why they were not), if you attended Yale University—regardless of what racial or ethnic or religious or gender group you are from—by this logic you would be complicit in imperialism. A degree from Yale means you've got blood on your hands. Whatever benefits your Yale degree gave you, it's time to give them back, or at least hand them over to someone else who did not attend Yale. And shame on you for taking advantage of imperialist privilege.

Or, and this is just a thought, we could realize how stupid it would be to hold graduates of Yale accountable for whatever Elihu Yale did back in the seventeenth-century (he did try to add a few regulations to the slave trade there to make it more humane, but still, he had no problem letting the slave trade continue). The Past and Present Test would make that very clear: we cannot hold someone accountable in the present for something that happened in the past. And that is important because so much of the animosity that gets churned up in the present in discussions about diversity is actually focused on the past. "You did this to my ancestors!" and so on. And yes, someone did do that to someone's ancestors, but not everyone did (which means it would also fail the General-Specific

Test), and even of those who did, none are alive today to face the consequences. If there is an act of racism, or discrimination, or prejudice, or any other ugly thing that happens here and now, then we need to call it out and make sure it never happens again, whether through the application of the law or through the application of ourselves to create a better sense of understanding. But we really cannot sustain anger in the present for the wrongdoings of the past, and to confuse the two, or to expect justice now for things that happened then, is to misuse and misapply the principles of diversity. Diversity fails for many reasons right now, and this obsession with judging the past through the present is one of the key areas where everything breaks down.

We can also apply this test, along with another, to approach one of the more controversial issues that relates to diversity, and that is the case for reparations for black Americans. In recent memory, this issue was given new life by author Ta-Nehisi Coates, in an article titled "The Case for Reparations," which appeared in *The Atlantic* in May 2014.[15] Such is the poverty of our dialogue on diversity that for some, merely questioning the idea of reparations in any way is twisted into being "pro-slavery" or racist or some other negative label. What we need here is rational thought, a way to make sense of the issue using an analytical tool-kit that isn't attached to identity.

One of the things that Coates has tried to do is to expand the charge sheet, as it were, of things for which reparations are due. It isn't just slavery, but all of the other things that are a legacy of slavery, including structural (or institutional) racism that persistently discriminates against blacks. Since my point here is to show how we can use these tests rather than to engage in a point-by-point

---

15 Ta-Nehisi Coates, "The Case for Reparations," *The Atlantic* (June 2014) at https://www.theatlantic.com/magazine/archive/2014/06/the-case-for-reparations/361631/

dialogue with Coates and others who have written on this issue, I'm not going to go into every single element that is involved in discussions on reparations. I should also point out that reparations are a *legal* issue, not a moral one. Next, I'll pull what might seem to be an unrelated example into the discussion to show how it helps to clarify the issue.

In any report on the human rights situation in North Korea from pretty much any organization that monitors activity in that country, there will be what is undoubtedly and justifiably a long list of documented human rights violations. Among those human rights violations one will always find the charge that North Korea engages in what is called collective punishment. If a North Korean citizen commits a crime, North Korea punishes not only the person who committed the crime, but also other people related to them. The entire family might be sent to a prison camp or punished in some other way, and more significantly for my purpose here, the guilt is applied over generations. By the standards of fair justice in human rights law, only the specific individual who committed the illegal act can be punished. Collective punishment is thus a human rights violation. In the context of the discussion on reparations, what this means is that the case for reparations over slavery fails both the *General-Specific Test*, because it holds one group collectively responsible for what only some did (collective punishment by presumed relation), and it also fails the *Past and Present Test*, because it attributes guilt to those in the present who have no connection to the harm done in the past (collective punishment over generations).

Note that I used the word "harm" rather than crime. I did so not to make slavery look less awful than it was, but because of another reason, one drawn straight from the field of law (and again, reparations are always a legal issue). In the field of law, whether domestic or international, there is a foundational principle that is known by its Latin name as *nullem crimen sine lege* (no crime without the law). What it means is that for something to be considered a crime, the law that rendered the act a criminal act had to be in force at the time of the commission of the act. In simpler terms, it means you cannot retroactively apply the law. So the question we have here is whether slavery was illegal at the time it was practiced in the United States, and the answer to that question is no. Slavery might be universally prohibited by human rights law now, in the present, but at that time in the past, it was not a crime, and by this particular legal principle, we cannot retroactively apply the law to hold people accountable. We therefore reach a contradiction that nullifies the argument for reparations for slavery. To take this one step further—and please understand I am not writing this with any sense of happiness—by the logic of the law, since reparations violate this foundational legal principle, reparations themselves would be an injustice.

If we bring the case for reparations into acts committed in the present, as Coates argues we should, we still don't get a clear answer. Note that in law, one cannot punish a "legacy" or a general experience—each specific crime is a separate act and must be considered separately. The kinds of questions we would have to answer to sustain the case for reparations for acts in the present are questions such as: (1) were only blacks targeted and harmed by the alleged institutional racism? (answer: no); (2) was the government that carried out the alleged acts exclusively white? (answer: no); (3) was the alleged systematic discrimination part of an official and explicit government policy that expressed the specific intent to discriminate against blacks (and only blacks)? (answer: no); (4) did all white citizens of the United States support and endorse the alleged acts of systematic discrimination? (answer: no).

In other words, even the other elements on the charge sheet fail the *General-Specific Test*, which means by default, the lingering and persistent sentiment against whites that clouds so much discourse on diversity itself fails the *Past and Present Test*. We can't hold an entire race accountable for what specific individuals did, past or present. The only thing we can do—and this is straight out of the fundamental principles of law—is to hold specific individuals accountable. The International Criminal Court (ICC), for instance, has asserted its jurisdiction over slavery as a crime against humanity and a war crime, but one important thing you should know about the ICC is this: *the ICC can only try and punish individuals*. The ICC cannot try an entire racial group, assuming somehow that all in the group are equally and collectively complicit, nor can it try an entire nation, assuming somehow that everyone in the country is complicit in and thus guilty of the alleged act. The reason it cannot do that is because both of those would violate the fundamental principles of law and justice. Those who advocate for reparations claim they are making demands for justice, but the reality is that reparations only give us more injustice when what we really need is less. If we can make diversity work and make it work collectively, with all of us involved equally, we might just get to the place where we really need to be, which is a place of no injustice.

Looking at diversity as a struggle between perpetrators and victims is a very unproductive way to obtain justice. It creates an erroneous belief that the work of diversity is the work of the alleged perpetrators. For the alleged victims of the perpetrators of injustice, the work of diversity is always *someone else's* work to do. I have discussed repeatedly in these chapters how the work of diversity is in fact always a shared responsibility, not something alleged perpetrators do in the service of alleged victims. I am offering these "tests" as a way to help us sort through the conflicting claims of injustice. The events of the past, however reprehensible they may be, do not change the responsibility we have in the present to make diversity work for us all.

Applying the tests
As I have said, none of these tests is absolutely foolproof, but at least they give us a common place to start, a fair and constructive foundation to improve upon. What we have in the present is an overabundance of divisive rhetoric, a panoply of coded or emotionally-charged words, that prevent us from achieving some type of shared perspective with which to see the same events, the same trends, and the same mistakes that undermine our current approaches to diversity. Will it be easy? Of course not—once again I need to point out that the work of diversity is difficult and arduous work, the burdens of which need to be borne by us all. Some people might balk at these tests, because as I said, too many people think that everyone else needs to change for diversity to work. Apply the test to *them*, not to me, they insist. That's a great idea, if our goal is never to solve anything and never to make an effort. But for diversity to work in a way that works for us all, we've all got to do something different. These tests can help us bravely craft a new world, without following the unsettling path of Aldous Huxley's *Brave New World*. The situation may seem dire and bleak, but we don't have to accept it as such. We ourselves are the solution we seek.

CHAPTER 5

REWARDING DIVERSITY

Perhaps the biggest obstacle that stands in the way of changing diversity from a game to a gain is the fact that all of the incentives we now have in place reward the box-checking and self-championing modes of identity. Everything rewards passive existence and almost nothing rewards active understanding. I could talk all day about how making the extra effort to achieve a new type of diversity, one based on personal ethics and civic responsibility, is something that pays handsome dividends to us all, but for many, that is an insufficient incentive for change. Just because something is an inherent good and just because it is the right thing to do, it still isn't enough to convince people that constructive change is what we need. So how might we incentivize the necessary revolution in diversity to move ourselves beyond the static and stale discussions we have right now, discussions that go nowhere and tend to leave us all frustrated and more divided than we were when we started talking? I'm all for rewarding diversity, so long as we are rewarding the right type of diversity. And by that I mean rewarding *efforts* rather than mere *existence*.

Diversity is open for business
One of the most fertile places for creating incentives for diversity is in the workplace. Employers are often under pressure to create or improve diversity, though often they have no idea what that really means. Partly in the absence of any meaningful guidelines for diversity, and partly because many identity-based groups advocate change along the lines of passive expressions of diversity (hire more Latinos, hire more Asians, hire more women, etc.), most companies end up playing the numbers game. Managers and employers often think like this: "We hired three Latinos this year—looks like we've got diversity." The problem that happens at the workplace, however, is that other employees often look at these new employees as "diversity hires," people who were not necessarily the most qualified candidates for their jobs but got them because the company was under pressure to "enhance" diversity. Even worse—and I know this because I have spent time conducting workshops for companies that are having problems with diversity—the various identity-based groups at the workplace often self-segregate into identity-based clusters, little enclaves at the workplace, leaving everyone confused if not resentful. There might be lots of diverse faces around the office, but at the same time, very little actual diversity to speak of.

Now let's look instead at the hiring process from the point of view of the type of *active* diversity I have been advocating all along the path of this journey, one based on the active effort to understand others rather than just promote and champion the passive characteristics of the self, and one that is more outward looking than inward looking. Let's imagine two candidates for the same job, and for simplicity's sake, let's assume that both are American citizens by birth.

The first candidate is a Muslim woman of Egyptian heritage. She has a degree from Stanford in business management with a 4.0 grade-point average. While she was a student, she took three years of Arabic, minored in Islamic Studies, spent a semester studying abroad in Egypt, and volunteered during all four years of her undergraduate studies at a local non-profit that helps female Muslim refugees in America.

The second candidate is a white male of Swedish heritage. He has a degree from Princeton in business management, also with a 4.0 grade point average. While he was an undergraduate student, he took three years of Thai, minored in Southeast Asian studies, spent a semester studying abroad in Kenya, and volunteered all four years teaching GED classes to prisoners at a state penitentiary.

With our current standards of diversity, we all know what the outcome would be. The "diverse" choice is to hire the Muslim woman. We think that diversity means bringing in more non-white people, and when that happens, we just hope that somehow, "diversity" will happen. Again, we might get a diverse set of faces at the workplace by this route, but we have no guarantee at all that this will lead to more tolerance, more understanding, more interaction, or a more productive work environment.

If we switch our standards to a more active approach to diversity, one that values the understanding of others more than the promotion of self, the white male actually turns out to be the candidate that will bring more meaningful diversity to the workplace. He challenged himself to learn a language that was not related to his cultural heritage, in order to understand something new and different, and then went on to study Southeast Asia, a place that was entirely unfamiliar to him before he began his studies at the university. When it came time to study abroad, he also challenged himself to enter a different cultural environment, in this case Kenya, to learn more about others and to challenge himself to learn new ways of doing things and viewing the world.

The woman, on the other hand, made nearly all of her choices based on her self and her community. Having already grown up in a Muslim family, she pursued Islamic studies as a minor to further entrench what she was already familiar with, and her choice to study in Egypt largely reflected a desire to "go back" and to spend time with extended family or to immerse herself further into a culture with which she was already familiar. There were a few challenges to living in Egypt perhaps, but cultural connections ensured a safe and smooth transition. Arabic was a language she heard growing up and could already speak, though not fluently, and even though Stanford offered dozens of other languages, she chose the one that was closest to her heritage. There seems very little desire to study and understand things that are outside her already familiar cultural environment, which means she is making much less of a contribution to diversity than the white male candidate.

If the company were truly interested in promoting diversity, they should value someone who has experience in learning new and different things, and one who has learned the craft of speaking across and between different cultural environments. Someone who has declined the diverse opportunities of education and has instead sought out familiarity and homogeneity has very little experience negotiating or communicating across the different parameters of identity. There is no reason to believe that this self-centered habit would change in the workplace either. If we are going to reward diversity as active understanding rather than passive existence, then the company in this case would hire the white male since he has made a far larger contribution to diversity than the Muslim woman. Note that they key word here is *contribution*, and not difference. We should value people based upon their active contribution to diversity (experience with inter-cultural understanding), not on their passive identity (being born into a non-dominant community). Diversity is not about bringing the *appearance* of difference into the workplace. It is about bringing the *understanding* of difference. Someone who is merely displaying their own identity will contribute far less to diversity in the workplace than someone who has devoted time to understanding the identities of others.

Right now, I am quite sure this suggestion seems counterintuitive, if not altogether absurd. But there are a number of benefits that flow from recalibrating our thinking in this direction. First of all, it takes the awkwardness out of the work environment that is generated by affirmative action and what is called diversity-based hiring. While few people would admit it openly, the practice of hiring people by appearance or by identity-category to create some sort of "diverse" work force—by which I mean hiring people that are non-white—creates an awkwardness that is felt by everyone, including the newly-hired employees. When these types of hiring practices occur under our current system of diversity, where we are valued more for our appearance than for our substance, people end up thinking, "Oh, you were hired because you are Latino," or "This is John, our new black employee" (think of the character Token on *South Park*, whose name satirizes the idea that having one black person in the office, or in the classroom, etc., shows that you have "diversity").

If you think I am exaggerating things or being cynical, I can assure you I'm not. All you need to do is spend some time reading job advertisements to see what I am talking about. What you will find are what are called *diversity tags*—messages embedded within the job description that will say things like "women and minorities are strongly encouraged to apply" or "persons from underrepresented minorities are strongly encourage to apply" or "our company is strongly committed to diversity." Yet none of these shows any valuation of the ability to negotiate and communicate across cultural lines, nor do they show any valuation of contributions to understanding difference. Applicants are valued simply because they are from a certain group. The word "underrepresented" in fact calls attention to how diversity has become simply a numbers game. We don't see people for what they are. We see people for the category they represent.

Let me return for a moment to our two hypothetical job candidates. As I discussed in earlier, one of the defenses one might hear from the Muslim woman candidate, for instance, about why she chose to go to Egypt to study abroad, where she still had extended family, would be something like this: "In my culture, family is very important," or, "America is very Islamophobic, so I wanted to go to a place where I could reconnect with my culture." These are nonsensical excuses that we need to reject, because they are predicated on the erroneous belief that somehow family is not important in other (American) cultures, or that the best response to perceived discrimination in America is to flee to other homogeneous cultural environments. It's really a backhanded insult to the white male candidate, as if to say, "of course you went to Kenya rather than Sweden, because white people always abandon their families." In reality, the white male made the more difficult choice, because even though family for him is just as important as it is for the Muslim woman candidate, he consciously made the choice to choose something different, to try to understand it and to struggle with difference. And hiring the sort of person who would make such a choice would make for a much more creative work environment—you know you have an employee who welcomes the challenge of something new and who is at ease dealing with all different types of people from all different walks of life. That makes him much better for diversity than a person who simply chose the narcissistic path of self-segregation and sameness.

One final reason why hiring the white male in this case would be the more diverse and better choice is that it would also create an incentive for other candidates to challenge themselves in similar ways. Once one employer, and then another and then another, makes it clear that there is a new type of diversity in town, that what is valued most of all is the effort to understand what is different rather than to posture about what is already familiar, it will create an entirely new incentive system to drag us out of the comfy confines of navel-gazing homogeneity and force us to come to terms with understanding the difference of others. Once that happens, when the next Muslim woman candidate comes along, perhaps she would have spent some time studying medieval Spanish literature, or volunteering at a Jewish charity, or perhaps she might have backpacked across Iceland, and with that type of skill set and outlook, she would be hired for her *contributions to diversity* and not for her membership in a group. The understanding and experience she has with truly different peoples and environments is what would be valued, rather than the fact that she can check the two boxes "Muslim" and "woman" on the diversity checklist. And other employees, hearing of the choices she has made and the different things she has studied and the different places she has been, would be far less inclined to think "she was hired because she is a Muslim woman" and far more inclined to say "she sounds like a really interesting person—I can't wait to get to know her and hear more of the things she has learned and done." There's far more dignity in that approach to diversity than anything we have produced so far.

Playing basketball with Oscar
Public displays of diversity are often highly valued for their symbolic capital. This is why you end up with people obsessing over the faces in the background of a candidate's political rally, and why candidates send their staff out into the crowd to hand-pick people who "look different" so they can appear in the background in what is a flagrant and also flagrantly artificial "display" of diversity. But let's veer away from politics for a moment and move instead toward the world of entertainment. In 2016, in response to the fact that no actors of color were nominated in any key category, the *#OscarsSoWhite* movement was born. Diversity activists quickly mobilized to put pressure on the Academy to "diversify," meaning

to include more women and minorities in the very elite group of people who make the decisions about who gets nominated for what and who actually wins the coveted Oscar. Given the very public nature of celebrity culture, the Academy scrambled to accommodate the demands for diversity as quickly as possible. Diversity activists applauded and everyone waited to see what would happen in 2017. Would diversity win?

Before I open the envelope to let you know if diversity won, let's take a moment to see what was actually happening. First, the assumption that was made in relation to the 2016 outcome was that having all white nominees in all the key categories was an act of racism created by a lack of diversity. It couldn't possibly have been that in that particular year, those nominees might have actually given the best performances. The corollary to this, however, is what shows the artifice of diversity. By diversifying the Academy with women and minorities, the expectation was that women and minorities would *necessarily* vote differently, that women would vote for women and minorities would vote for minorities. Imagine what would have happened if the Academy had "enhanced" its diversity, and then returned yet another slate of all white nominees. It would be the outcome *that could not happen*. If it did, the women and minorities who diversified the Academy would be excoriated and ostracized by their communities. *How could a person of color vote for a white person?* White members of the Academy can vote for whomever they want, it seems, but there is an expectation that women and minorities could not and should not do the same. They vote for themselves—identity is destiny. Diversity has thus created differential treatment and differential expectations, when what it's supposed to provide is equality.

And of course, in opening the envelope at last, I can say that diversity did indeed win. Or did it? The next day after the Oscars, as I sat in a café near campus, I overheard a conversation about the awards ceremony, and when the conversation turned to the fact that *Moonlight* had won the award for Best Picture, one person among them said "Well, they didn't really have a choice, did they?" For clarity, this was in liberal Berkeley, and the person who said that was not white. I find the statement very depressing. *Moonlight* is actually an excellent film, but the push for diversity created a situation where, at least in the minds of some, it won because the Academy was under pressure to "showcase" diversity. As is often the case in many a workplace, diversity created an outcome that seemed awkwardly artificial.

So much for the Oscars. Now I'm going to switch over to another very public area of activity and get a bit more hypothetical. With the Oscars, the clamor for diversity was based on the idea that diversity was always a good thing and no matter where we look, we should strive to promote more diversity. Yet I can think of one public area of activity where not only is no one clamoring for diversity, but also if someone did, there would probably be protests in the streets. What am I talking about here? I'm talking about the world of professional sports.

Let's take a look, for instance, at the National Basketball Association, otherwise known as the NBA. According to The Institute for Diversity and Ethics in Sport (TIDES), located in the College of Business Administration at the University of Central Florida, the diversity breakdown of NBA players in 2014 was 19.5% white and 77% black. That means that *all* other minority groups represented only 3.5% of the NBA. *Clearly there is a diversity problem in the NBA*, and yet, unlike the Oscars, no one is saying anything. Seriously, who's your favorite Latino NBA player? Can't think of one? The good news is that the numbers changed a bit for 2015, with white players coming in at 23.3% and black players at 74.4%, but the bad news is that the percentage of NBA players from *all other ethnic groups* went down to 2.3%. So where is the outcry for diversity? And I haven't even discussed the issue of gender disparity yet—the Women's National Basketball Association (WNBA) has generated very little interest among viewers and has salaries and budgets that are nowhere near what men earn.

One might be tempted to say that blacks are simply better athletes, and yet we can no more say that than we can say, for instance, that whites are simply better actors which is why so many get nominated. With the Oscars, we assume that all identity groups are equally talented, and therefore if the percentages of membership in the Academy or the percentages of nominees does not reflect the overall percentages of these groups in the general population, then discrimination has occurred and more diversity is needed. At universities, we make the assumption that all identity groups are equally intelligent, and therefore if the percentage of student attendance does not reflect overall percentages of these groups in the general population, then discrimination has occurred and more diversity is needed. So why don't we make the same assumption for professional sports? Diversity tells us that we're all equally talented, but the percentages for NBA players are grotesquely skewed, so isn't it time to "diversify" the NBA?

Let's take a look hypothetically to see what this would look like, and let's assume we want to get this in place before next season, as with the Oscars. With the numbers game approach to diversity, the argument is that people should be represented at roughly the same percentage their groups have in the general population. African-Americans are roughly 13% of the population, so they're going to take a big hit when we diversify the NBA (but that's okay, because diversity asks us all to make sacrifices). Latinos are around 17%, so teams will have to scramble to hire as many Latino players as they can as quickly as they can. Asians are 6% so the same holds true for this group as well. Perhaps in the name of equity and inclusion (both are diversity buzzwords) we can fold the WNBA into the NBA, aiming for gender parity.

The Golden State Warriors just won the title for 2017, so let's take a look to see what the starting line-up will look like for the

2018 season, based on our current approach to diversity. We've got 5 people on the team, so in the name of diversity, we'll have one black player, one white player, one Latino player, one Asian player, and one player from any of the other underrepresented categories. At least two of the players will be women, and possibly three, if we really want to promote diversity and shatter some glass ceilings. However, it's not even as straightforward as that. About half-way into the first quarter, we'll have to start making substitutions. There are lots of different Asian groups in the US, for example, so in the interest of diversity we'll have to start rotating them in—the Chinese-American player comes out and we send in the Lao-American player, only to yank him out in the second quarter and put in the Nepali-American, and so forth. And I haven't even touched on how we'll rotate in persons from the LGBTQI+ community.

I could go on, but I think I've made the point quite clearly. We all know what would happen. *No one would watch this.* There would be protests *against* diversity, and *#StopNBAdiversity* would be the new hashtag. So why are we okay with this? If diversity makes everything better, wouldn't it make the NBA better, too? The whole point of this comparative exercise is to show how foolish it is to turn diversity into a numbers game. Whether it's the Oscars or the NBA, "percentage monitoring" does nothing to enhance our understanding of each other. It just takes us back to putting different people in the same room and saying that somehow, diversity happened. It didn't happen. Nothing happened. We shouldn't be looking at percentages and we shouldn't be looking for ways to "showcase" diversity, since it gives us appearance without substance. Neither the *#OscarsSoWhite* campaign nor my hypothetical diversification of the NBA gives us any sort of meaningful diversity. Clearly, we need something different, something more.

The failure of diversity in Hollywood isn't an issue of numbers. To my mind, there's no better example of the failure of diversity in Hollywood than the fact that people feel questions like, "Is it really appropriate for a white director to make a movie about a black topic?" are considered legitimate questions to ask. (Indeed, by my newly-proposed definition of racism, the question itself is racist.) Think, for instance, of the 1995 film *Sense and Sensibility*, adapted from the Jane Austen novel of the same name. To put it in brutally honest terms, the film depicts a world that is *extraordinarily* white, and yet the film was directed by Taiwan-born director Ang Lee. Was the film therefore inauthentic? Was it bad? Did Ang Lee culturally appropriate white culture? Actually the film went on to win many awards, including Best Picture at the Academy Awards in 1996. What the film shows us is precisely the kind of diversity we need. Encouraging directors and actors to move *away* from using art to promote their identity and *toward* using art to promote cross-cultural understanding is precisely what we need. Ang Lee shows how it can be done. Putting out a call for white directors to take on black topics, Chinese directors to take on white topics, black directors to take on Latino topics, and so forth, will push us into a much more substantive kind of diversity than merely monitoring numbers to make sure that 13% of Academy Award winners are African-American.

Educating ourselves in diversity
Something similar could be implemented at universities and other schools at all levels of education. Most universities have study abroad programs, and most of them require an application, and so universities could easily prioritize those students who want to pursue the chance to study abroad—prioritize in terms of acceptance and financial assistance—who are using the experience to broaden their horizons and explore something different. The white male student who wants to go to Kenya, the Muslim female student who wants to go to Iceland, the African-American student who wants to go to South Korea—these would receive much higher priority

than for instance the Muslim female student who wants to go to Jordan or the Korean-America student who wants to go to South Korea. The latter two choices, for instance, reflect very low contributions to diversity and a lack of desire to understand the difference of others. They should not be prioritized at all. This would build an educational incentive for students to use the wonderful opportunities they have at their disposal—studying abroad is only one example of this—to engage in an active form of diversity rather than just run around campus and around the world looking for familiarity and homogeneity. That kind of self-directed narcissism is the opposite of what diversity requires, and as such, should not be rewarded, supported, or prioritized.

Some might argue that none of this applies to those who are studying or are employed in what are often called the "hard sciences"—engineering, medicine, biology, and so forth. But diversity shows up pretty much everywhere there are people, it just sometimes shows up in different ways. In the medical sciences, for instance, there are all sorts of ways to apply one's medical skills in diverse ways, both domestically and internationally. I often hear students who are studying to become doctors tell me they want to "serve their communities," which means for instance that if they are of Korean-heritage they want to help Koreans, or if they are Latino they want to work with and help other Latinos. But if we really want to encourage diversity—an active type of diversity rather than a passive one—we would be encouraging the Korean-heritage doctor to work in the Latino community, or the Latino doctor to work in the Korean community, or any other such arrangement that again, encourages us to understand difference.

If a Korean doctor is asked to work in a Latino community, for instance, she will learn a wealth of knowledge in this new environment of active diversity. *First*, she might suddenly become aware that while she knows Korean and English, she doesn't know a word of Spanish. Having always thought that Spanish was "somebody else's language," she becomes aware that knowing Korean is a self-directed choice, and thus understands the importance of making other-directed choices.

Second, while working in the Korean community would earn her endless praise in the artificially homogeneous environment she has chosen—"We are so proud of you, being a doctor!" or "It's so nice you came back to serve your community"—working in the Latino community would allow her to understand that exclusion and discrimination are not just something that white people do, as she watches Latino patients avoid her and go elsewhere in search of Latino doctors. In other words, she would have to confront the challenges of a truly diverse environment and find a way to understand the patients with whom she interacts in her new community. She learns difference and also learns that prejudice and discrimination are universal in all communities.

Third, the patients in the Latino community are also forced to confront their own prejudicial preferences and search for a way to accept and trust an "outsider" to their community. When Latinos see a Korean name go up on the clinic staff board, and find themselves avoiding that doctor and going in search of a Spanish-speaking Latino doctor, at some point, they will have to confront the fact that they have plenty of racism in their own community. Racism isn't "out there" somewhere, being inflicted by a white man against someone else, it is right there in the heart of the Latino community, just as it is at the heart of every community—if you know where to look for it—and having more and more non-Latinos working in the Latino community is one of the best ways to overcome that racism. That's not gentrification—that's diversity.

Fourth, watching Latino patients seek out and prefer Latino doctors should make her reflect on her own first choice—to be a Korean doctor in the Korean community—and reflect on how that choice, too, is racist in its own way (or at least strongly prejudicial).

Perhaps then she would try to recruit Latino doctors to work in the Korean community, realizing right away that none of those Latino doctors know any Korean (for them, Korean is "someone else's language") and realizing that the Korean people in the Korean community would shun Latino doctors to seek out only Korean doctors. That kind of awareness, and those kinds of experiences, will help us push diversity into something new, something active, something inter-cultural, and something that works better for all of us.

I realize that for many people, studying at Stanford or Princeton or backpacking through Iceland or even becoming a doctor all sound more like a very privileged playground than an exercise in diversity, so I also want to emphasize that anyone can engage in this kind of diversity, wherever you live, whoever you are, and whatever you can afford, even if it is nothing at all. As I have said repeatedly, diversity is a state of mind, a demeanor, a way of seeing the world, and those kinds of things don't necessarily cost money. They are about the choices we make, not about the money we spend. Every time we walk out the door, we enter a world where choices are possible, a world where we can make some type of choice that makes a better diversity for all of us. The daughter of a poor coal-mining family in West Virginia who chooses to spend an hour after school at the public library reading a book on Japan, or the African-American child in Detroit who chooses to watch a documentary on Navajo music, have both made choices that are far more powerful acts of diversity than the Chinese-American father in San Francisco who spends his time trying to get his son enrolled in a Chinese-language school in Chinatown. Creating a new era of diversity—one that actually works and one that focuses on substantive understanding rather than narcissistic preening—really comes down to the choices we make. If diversity fails to deliver on its promise, it is because we have chosen poorly, and we really have no one but ourselves to blame.

The new checklist
Whether it is at the office or on campus, we need to alter everything we currently use to "monitor" diversity to make way for a new approach that gives us substance over appearance. Take, for instance, the dreaded box we all have to check to identify ourselves on pretty much everything we fill out or apply for. Some of the categories are downright bizarre. Caucasian, for instance, often includes people with heritages from Western Europe, Eastern Europe, the Middle East, and North Africa. That's right, a person whose heritage is Armenian, a person whose heritage is Libyan, a person whose heritage is Bosnian, and a person whose heritage is Swedish are considered pretty much the same thing. Some categories are either too simplistic, such as Black, while mixed race people are often told to choose whichever identity is "dominant." (Seriously?) My favorite identity category is Other, which is apparently the most diverse and confused identity group in the world. Some forms now list "Decline to State," but just so you know, in my experience, if you check that box, it is assumed you are white and are trying to mask your privilege.

So how might we completely reconceive this whole approach to identity, the box-based approach to diversity? One way to do it would be to rephrase the question and completely change the possible answers. Instead of "please choose one of the following" from a list of boxes where you have one choice of category, why not rephrase the question to something like this: "which of the following three categories have been most influential in your life?" Instead of the five or six options now offered, we could expand the list to include dozens of different things. There could be India, Nepal, Mongolia, Islam, Catholicism, Bolivia, and so on. We could even include Gender, but without specifying an actual gender (the point being that gender was significant in how you perceive your identity, which could be true for male, female, or transgender). The responses wouldn't be ranked, either. There would just be three (or perhaps five) boxes that you check—the important influences that made you who you are.

The first benefit we would get from such an approach is that anyone looking at your application will have no idea what your specific heritage or ethnicity is, which means they can make no assumptions about who you are. Moreover, for those who sit on hiring or admissions committees, what you have in front of you is not, as we currently have, a solitary box to match with percentages to facilitate the numbers-game style of diversity, but rather an interesting array of different influences that offer a more complex description of who a person is. An unexpected combination of things, for instance, would reveal a better experience with substantive diversity. This approach would reward applicants who sought out and worked in different and unfamiliar environments, as opposed to those who simply check "Latino" and then hope the company or school wants more Latinos. The new approach rewards those who interact with and understand others, instead of rewarding people who merely "stick with their own kind."

At universities, we could set up a system whereby students earn what might be called a Diversity Contribution Score. Students earn points when they engage in activities that force them to experience new and different things, and they need to earn a certain number of points, let's say 10, before they can graduate. If a university or a department has a foreign language requirement—and all of them should—the language a student chooses will translate into a certain number of points. A Korean-American student who takes Korean, for instance, might earn 1 point or perhaps even 0 points. If the Korean-American student takes Swahili or Tamil, however, the student may get 5 points. We should also eliminate the possibility of "testing out" of a language, since the language a student tests out in is invariably their heritage language, and thus they also "test out" of and bypass diversity.

We could do the same with breadth requirements as well. A Russian-American student who takes Russian history for a breadth requirement gets 1 point or 0 points, whereas if she takes African history she gets 3 or 4 points. We could apply this system to study abroad programs, on-campus activities, and pretty much everything else related to the educational experiences that a university is supposed to provide. A system like this would reward students for pursuing substantive diversity, walking in the shoes of others, and help us break free from the current system in which students are encouraged to seek out "their own kind" and learn about themselves rather than about others.

Similar systems could be worked out for the workplace as well. This is just a place to start—so many directions we could go from here. The main point is that we need to completely rethink everything we are now doing in relation to diversity, because we are doing it wrong. We don't need more of what we are now doing. We need instead something completely different. That, to reiterate one more time, has been my whole point all along this journey.

The new heroes of diversity
I would never have written these words if I didn't think diversity were a worthwhile pursuit, if I didn't think it were salvageable from the mess it's currently in, if I didn't think it could be refashioned into something new and something wonderful. I think I have made it clear that it is possible, just as I have also made it clear that this is going to take a lot of work—work that we all need to share equally. Employers can do their fair share by creating a whole new system of incentives for potential job candidates (and for current employees for that matter), and schools and universities can do the same. We ought to be rewarding those who opened new doors and walked through them, not those who remained behind their own doors and found comfort among "their people." Along with these new incentives we need a new crop of everyday heroes—unexceptional

people who have made exceptional choices—to pave the way and show how it can be done. Under our current regime of diversity, if a university wants to hire new faculty, an African-American who studies African-American things and an Indian woman who studies Indian women are considered to be "good choices" for diversity—authentic in their identities and diverse merely by their existence. But an African-American man studying African-American things, or an Indian woman studying Indian women, or an Asian-American studying Asian-American politics—what they all have in common is same-to-same connections, and a same-to-same connection reflects homogeneity and narcissism, and thus a *lack* of diversity. For diversity, we need same-to-different connections built on understanding and the development of trust. We need the Korean doctor in the Latino community, the Indian woman studying African-American history, or the African-American man studying Inuit language and literature, or the West Virginia coal miner's daughter reading Ngugi wa Thiong'o after school, or the Choctaw child studying Italian cooking. Those and others like them are the new heroes of diversity.

Creating a new diversity also means acknowledging things that hitherto no one has cared or dared to acknowledge. We need to tear down the myths and fantasies we currently believe in, such as the idea that racism is something that only white people can inflict on others, and we need to understand and admit the reality that racism comes and goes from and to all directions and all communities. We need to acknowledge and confront what I have called the new face of racism. No longer is racism just the white man with the sinister grin making racist remarks behind closed doors. It's that, true, but it's also far more than that. It's anything or anyone that encourages us or forces us to think and see in racialized ways. There is racism and prejudice and discrimination and narcissism and hatred anywhere you look in America, and so far our regime of diversity has done almost nothing to make it better and almost nothing to make it stop. We need something new and we need something better, and we need to demand it from ourselves as much as we demand it from others. And yes, I'm enough of a fool to think it can actually happen, just as I am enough of a realist to fear for the future of America if it doesn't.

EPILOG

UNPOISONING THE WELL

In the afternoon of April 15, 2013, on the edge of Boylson Street in downtown Boston, a group of runners headed toward Copley Square and toward the finish line of the Boston Marathon. Suddenly, two loud and percussive explosions etched their sinister signature onto the urban soundscape. Up until that moment, just before three o'clock in the afternoon, the only sounds that one could hear were the rhythmic patter of running shoes on the pavement, the encouraging cheers of onlookers who cheered the runners on for the final stretch, and the gentle flapping of the flags that stood in a row alongside the street to represent the international crowd that had gathered that day, both to compete and to observe. There was confusion, fear, bravery, and defiance in the aftermath of the twin bombings, which occurred on Patriots' Day in the civic calendar of Massachusetts. The wake of those horrific blasts left three people dead and over 260 others injured, many of them severely.

An investigation quickly followed, and soon authorities were able to name two suspects as the culprits behind this atrocity—Dzhokar and Tamerlan Tsarnaev. Dzhokar and Tamerlan were brothers in a family that had immigrated to the United States from the troubled region of Chechnya in Russia. The two brothers came from a Muslim family, and at least initially, had settled peacefully into their new lives in America. Whatever happened in the course of building their new lives in America, and however it happened, on April 15, 2013, it had become clear that something had gone horribly off course in all of that. According to the preliminary investigations, the two brothers wanted to kill as many Americans as they could and wreak as much damage and havoc as possible. In the manhunt that followed the bombings, the elder brother Tamerlan was eventually killed in a shootout with police, while the younger brother Dzhokar escaped and continued to evade arrest until he was discovered, hiding in a boat under a tarp, on the evening of April 19. As Dzhokar lay in his hiding place, he found a pen and began to write a few things on the interior of the boat, since he could find no paper. Among the things he wrote that evening was a simple phrase that was short, blunt, and angry: "Fu*k America." (I've slightly edited the original F-bomb.)

It's a juvenile scribbling, I admit, but there is still something that defies explanation to chart the course that goes from the day that Dzhokar Tsarnaev acquired his American citizenship on September 11, 2012—a day that will always be an emotional and somber one for America—to the day just seven months later when he was hiding in a boat, after allegedly participating in yet another moment of terrorist infamy, scribbling words of condemnation about his newly adopted country. The question of "what went wrong?" was on everyone's mind, as it still is today and probably will be for some time to come. A number of tentative answers have been offered since then, some of which deal with the personal issues of Dzhokar and Tamerlan and the Tsarnaev family, and some of which deal with larger issues about the identity of America. My goal here is not to write about the personal stories and motives of Dzhokar and Tamerlan Tsarnaev, but I am specifically interested in how we might be able to make sense of what happened in Boston by looking more closely at diversity in America. I wouldn't argue that the Boston Bombings were somehow the direct outcome of the failure of diversity in America—that would be too facile an argument to make. But I would say that the tragedy of the Boston Bombings can serve as a somber reminder to all of us of why it is so important to take diversity seriously, to understand ourselves among others, and to make diversity work in a way that gives us all a sense of belonging. In one way or another, we all have a stake in making diversity work.

One of the more trite and cliché answers that is often offered as to why there is so much animosity against America, and here the reference is specifically to the various Islamic terrorist groups that claim they want to destroy America, is that "they hate us because of our freedom." I understand how this answer offers a certain amount of smug satisfaction for Americans but at the same time I understand how it also frustrates more than it resolves because it is a statement that has very little substance behind it. It makes little sense to want to kill someone because they are free, and the idea that somewhere out there, whether in America or elsewhere in the world, there are people who are murderously angry because Americans have a lot of freedom, is something that cries out for more evidence and a better explanation. I won't claim to have solved the whole thing, but I can at least shed a little light on the meaning of that freedom and why the anger it generates is so misplaced.

When I spoke about the American Dream so many pages ago, I stated that the American Dream is a right to have a dream, to imagine a different future and to imagine the path it would take to get there. The American Dream is not the right to have your dream come true—America does not owe you an apology or compensation if your dream does not come true—nor is it the right to have whatever every other American has. It is a dream that is a personal dream, and American freedom, to give it a more substantive meaning, is the freedom to dream whatever it is you want to dream. That personal freedom also carries with it personal responsibility—freedom and responsibility are always mutually linked—and that is precisely where things link back to this idea about why "they hate us for our freedom."

In an angry rant that occurred in the aftermath of the Boston Bombings, and in the aftermath of the death of Tamerlan and the arrest of Dzhokar, the mother of the two brothers denounced America and claimed that the family came to America for democracy but that democracy had failed them. The reality however is that democracy did not fail the two brothers. Rather, the two brothers failed democracy. Not only that, but the "antidote" the two supposedly turned to in order to save themselves from the evils and temptations of American democracy—religious extremism and a violent Islamic *jihad*—actually ended up coming down on the side of American democracy. For anyone who cares to take a closer look, the two things that are normally considered implacable and irreconcilable enemies—American democracy and Islamic *jihad*—are actually allies that should, if done properly, end up moving in the same direction. If you are wondering how that could possibly be the case, then stay tuned for what's on next.

First, we need to understand this much-maligned and much-misunderstood concept of *jihad*. There are plenty of people out there who believe that *jihad* is a word that means "death to America" or "kill infidels" and all sorts of other ramblings that come from the mouths of people with mush-brained minds. But *jihad* actually means something quite different. The linguistic roots of the word *jihad*—and I am sorry to have to wax linguistic for just a moment—are linked with the idea of struggle or effort. Yes, I understand that for those who think that God put us here on earth just to kill each other, that effort (*jihad*) is seen as a blank check from God, one to be cashed after death in some imagined paradise, to blow others up and kill them. And yes, I understand

Unpoisoning the Well

that one of the meanings of *jihad* is indeed holy war. But that is only one of the meanings of *jihad*, and in spite of the saturation of much of the American press with the idea that *jihad* is synonymous with holy war—again not factually incorrect but definitely theologically misleading—the meaning of *jihad* that most Muslims are familiar with, whether in America or anywhere else in the world, is the effort or struggle that one makes as a Muslim to live one's life in accordance with the sacred guidelines offered by Islam. It is no different from the struggle to be a better Christian, or the struggle to be a better Buddhist, or the struggle to be a better Jew, or the struggle to be a better adherent of whatever one's faith may be. (If you are an atheist then just secularize the thought and if you are an anarchist and think you are not bound by any rules then you are not really an anarchist—you're a moron.) And here is the part that is important to know: in this context, *jihad* is a personal struggle, not a communal one.

In the latter sense, the essence of *jihad* is a lot like American freedom—it is a personal struggle, a personal choice, and a personal responsibility. If we add to that yet another stipulation of Islam (as in, a guiding principle of Islam for Muslims to follow), namely that there must be no compulsion in matters of faith (which is why one cannot be forced to convert to Islam, as the lack of free choice undermines the validity of the conversion), then it would seem that the more free the environment is, the more meaningful and substantive is the *jihad* to be a better Muslim. I know there are many people out there who think the answer to creating better Muslims is to eliminate all possible distractions, seclude Muslims (especially women) in their homes, and create an entirely homogeneous environment where everything in public and private life is Islamic. But without the element of choice and without the freedom to stray from the path, keeping to the path—engaging in the *jihad* to be a better Muslim—loses its meaning. So to a certain extent, "they" (if by "they" we mean those who want to segregate and control the Islamic community through violence) really do hate "us" (Americans) for our freedom because they no doubt understand at some level that only the freedom of democracy can create true faith and belief, a statement that is as true for Islam as it is for any religion. If they really thought things through, those who invoke religion—in this case Islam—in the endeavor to see America destroyed and to see Americans killed would reconsider their stance. If they are trying to create an environment where Muslims can be the best adherents of the faith they can be, they would be protecting America, not trying to destroy it. And as for the Tsarnaev brothers, to the extent that they lost their way and then blamed others and blamed America for getting lost, not only did they fail American democracy, but they also failed their *jihad*.

Keeping the faith in America
I haven't spoken much about religion in all these pages, and quite frankly that would take a whole separate book to deal with. Religion is one of the trickier parts of human identity—on the one hand, faith involves belief and belief is always the product of voluntary choice, yet at the same time, most of us follow the religion into which we were born, which would mean that we never really gave much thought to, or weren't allowed to give much thought to, any alternatives in the marketplace of spirituality. That is as true for Christianity as it is for pretty much every other religion in America, and I am aware that this is a very sensitive topic. If I were to recommend that we include the Navajo version of the creation of the universe in American schools, for example, there are many people who would oppose this, on the grounds that they don't want their children exposed to other belief systems. It might "confuse" them, or worse, it might make them want to convert.

But here, too, a diversity based on understanding can go a long way to create social peace in a multi-religious environment. I can understand the Navajo view of the creation of the universe, just as

I can understand the theological elements that make up any religion I care to study. If I were an atheist, at least it would help me to respect and understand those who choose to lead a life of faith, and if I were one who had already chosen a spiritual path, knowing the paths of others should not make me doubt my own, at least not if my faith is as deep and strong as it should be. The one thing I can be truly grateful for, regardless of what faith I may choose to hold, is that in America I am free to retain the one I have, to choose a new one if it appeals to me, or simply leave the old one behind and live a life where I question or doubt everything. I've been to many other places in the world where such choices are not possible, and people generally tend to be quite unhappy in those places. I don't care how pithy it sounds to say it, but American freedom is a rare species of freedom indeed, and taking it for granted or dismissing it as so much hypocrisy is the bulwark of buffoonery.

Fundamentally ourselves
Every time I start talking about faith, freedom, and democracy, I am reminded of a wonderful little film, based on a short story of the same name by Hanif Kureishi, called *My Son the Fanatic* (1997). The film revolves around various events in the lives of a family of Pakistani origin who have settled in Britain. Given the enhanced personal freedom offered by the social norms of Britain, as opposed to the more restrictive ones they experienced in Pakistan, the father in the family, who earns his living as a taxi driver, begins to explore new things and meet new people outside of the Pakistani community. He takes a liking to jazz, for instance, and ends up befriending and protecting a prostitute after she suffers a violent attack from a client.

In the meantime, the man's son has reacted to the freedom of Britain in the opposite direction, by denouncing the freedom as evil and by moving closer and closer to the "fundamentalist" aspects of the culture he left behind in Pakistan. In essence, the son wants the training wheels put back on, and he demands that they be put on for everyone else in the community as well, especially his father, whose behavior he finds outrageous. For the father, stepping away from the community and from the enclave, meeting and understanding new people, has transformed him into a new person, a person he clearly thinks is a better version of himself than he had in the less free environment of his homeland. He has embraced his new life, free of the training wheels that held him back. The son, on the other hand, wants to seal up the boundaries around the enclave—build a wall, so to speak—and recreate the world they left behind, even going so far as to denounce the "evils" of Britain, though of course he wants to stay in the country for the benefits it provides. By the end of the film, the father is not only willing to step away from the community and the enclave, but even to step away from his family, in order to cultivate a better sense of self. There is a not-so-thinly-veiled suggestion in the film that the father, though he appears to have drifted away from the strict Islamic values of the community of his birth, has in fact moved closer to the essence of those values through his personal choices and actions, while the son, though he appears to have embraced his pious Islamic values as a way to return to the faith, has in fact only done so superficially, as a form of posturing in the community.

Another work that brings a fresh perspective to the relationship between freedom and identity is the wonderful novel by Michael Ondaatje called *Anil's Ghost* (2000). If the author's name sounds familiar it is because he is also the author of *The English Patient*, probably his most well-known work, largely due to the film of the same name that was based on the book and that was hated so deeply by Elaine Benes. But *Anil's Ghost* is a different sort of novel, one that deals specifically with the question of identity. In the novel, Anil Tissera, a native Sri Lankan who has left her homeland to pursue her studies in Britain and America, is now returning to Sri Lanka.

Anil, a woman with a man's name (that she took from her brother), is returning to Sri Lanka but is traveling on a United Nations passport. She has come back to Sri Lanka to investigate claims of human rights violations in the midst of Sri Lanka's bloody civil war. On the outside, it appears that she is returning "home," but Anil realizes on arrival that Sri Lanka is now for her a foreign country. She has carved out her own life-path in Britain and in America, and the violence of the civil war in Sri Lanka, a civil war based entirely on disputes over identity, appalls her. Upon her arrival in Sri Lanka, all of her remaining family and friends want her to return to and embrace her community, in essence to take "their" side in the civil war, but she decides instead to remain who she is as an individual, which quickly creates mistrust among her family and her community. Eventually she ends up engaged in the task of trying to identify a skeleton unearthed from a grave to determine if the person whose skeleton it is may have been the victim of a war crime. The skeleton becomes a mirror for her own reconstructed sense of self, as she realizes that for all the violence of the Sri Lankan civil war, for all the importance put on sticking to one's own kind and never leaving one's community, underneath it all—we are all pretty much the same. Though the central characters in the investigation face extreme pressure to align their loyalties and prejudices with their ethnic and religious communities, the inner circle of friends—who come to understand that they have been "citizened by their friendship"—realize that when the unthinking loyalty to identity-based communities takes precedence over the commitment to ethics and justice, the result is division, violence, atrocity, and war.

I mention this novel, as I have mentioned Hanif Kureishi's work, in the context of discussing religion and democracy, because I want to bring this all back to that sad and tragic afternoon in Boston in April 2013. I know there are people in the United States, just as there are people elsewhere in the world, who think there are identities that are truly and intrinsically irreconcilable. I know that in the United States there are those who think that Islam and democracy are incompatible, but as I hope I have shown, that is not even close to the truth. There are no such things as incompatible identities, and if there is one thing that America ought to be able to prove to the world, it is at least that. My point in all of this, however, has been to show that the mere coexistence of Islam with democracy, or of Christians with Buddhists, or of Koreans with Japanese, or of Russians with Latinos, or of blacks with whites, is never enough. Mere coexistence won't do. It takes the extra step and the constant work to craft the kind of mutual understanding that diversity needs in order to thrive. America may be the improbable country, but it is not the impossible country—all it takes is a bit of guts, grit and gumption from all of us. America isn't someone else's country to repair, and diversity isn't someone else's responsibility to fix. It's us, here and now, and there's a lot left to do.

The new stories of diversity
In an earlier chapter, I discussed the idea of "happy slave" narratives, in which stories of exploitation and violence carried out by persons of color against other persons of color are distorted into positive narratives of community and empowerment. The current state of diversity creates an environment in which injustice, oppression, exploitation, and racism can only be inflicted by whites, and non-whites can only be victims of those things. I have tried to show how destructive this perspective is for the whole platform of diversity, and how it creates a misplaced mistrust that needs to be removed before meaningful justice can be obtained. I also argued that if diversity is going to provide equality, part of that equality has to be what I called negative equality—equal scrutiny of our pasts and presents to rewrite a new critical history of everything.

If you think that sounds like so much cloud-gazing idealism, or if you simply have no idea what that might look like, the good news is that a few others have gotten the message and we do have a few pioneers to help blaze a new trail for a new diversity. One eloquent example of what I am talking about is the beautifully-written essay by Alex Tizon entitled "My Family's Slave," published in the June 2017 issue of *The Atlantic*. Tizon, a Pulitzer Prize-winning, Filipino-American journalist, had tried for years to get the story published, but it was precisely the kind of story that no one wanted to hear—one that dared to suggest that people of color were not always innocent victims of history.[16] Sadly, when *The Atlantic* finally decided it was time to let the story be told, they tried to contact Tizon to say that the story was a go, only to learn that Tizon had passed away earlier that very day.

Tizon's essay is actually the story of a woman named Eudocia Tomas Pulido, whom Tizon knew only as Lola. Lola was a live-in servant, brought to America by Tizon's family for the purpose of being their servant, who raised Tizon and his siblings and took care of all the chores in the house for 56 years, all of it without pay. Tizon's essay is partly a paean to Lola, to tell a story of a life that might otherwise have been forgotten. But it is also partly the tale of how Tizon ultimately comes to realize that Lola, this unpaid servant who had lived with him and his family all those years, was really a household slave. When she came to live with Tizon in 1999, this realization slowly dawned on him. In his own words: "I had a family, a career, a house in the suburbs—the American dream. And then I had a slave."

The article has generated quite a bit of discussion, as rightfully it should. I don't want to spend time analyzing all of the reactions as much as point out that the reactions do hint at what a different diversity might look like, can look like, should look like. Some of the response has consisted of the same kind of rhetoric I talked about

---

16 Alex Tizon, "My Family's Slave," *The Atlantic* (June 2017) at https://www.theatlantic.com/magazine/archive/2017/06/lolas-story/524490/

earlier when I referenced "happy slave" narratives. Some Filipinos and Filipino-Americans referred to the keeping of unpaid laborers as a "cultural practice," or a part of Filipino "tradition." Tizon was wrong to use the world "slave," they said, as it made the practice sound negative. On the other hand, when several non-Filipino critics rebuked Tizon for trying to extricate himself from his own complicity in Lola's exploitation, it created a strange community-based defense of Tizon against these critical "Westerners," who apparently had no right to say anything critical about a culture that was not their own. Sadly, all of this pushed Lola even further from the center of what was in essence her own life story. None of this should really come as much of a surprise—it's the standard, unproductive quibbling that our current approach to diversity always serves up.

But there were a few other voices that saw Tizon's narrative for what it was. A warts-and-all revelation about Filipino history and the Filipino-American experience that showed a very different and critical perspective that the current myths of diversity keep suppressing. It's a breakthrough moment, one in which we realize that looking back into the past is going to be a painful process for all of us, not just for some of us. The fact that some people are ready to see something new, ready to see things differently than the standard "white" (guilty) versus "people of color" (innocent) narratives shows that we are possibly on the verge of a new revolution, a new diversity that finally unites us, rather the diversity we now have, which always divides us. We need more narratives like Tizon's, and we all need to read them and understand them for what they are.

Why there's nothing else to do
I wonder at times if the well of American democracy has already been irreparably poisoned by the divisive politics of identity that have slowly seeped in through the ruins of a failed and collapsed system of diversity. For far too long, we have been enamored with

the idea that diversity was just all of us existing in our separate and different worlds, never venturing into each other's space, and spending far too much time cultivating pride in our own communities to cultivate an understanding of someone else's. Even more simplistically, there are still those who think that diversity is pushing down whites and pulling up non-whites. I think the division and anger and mistrust that saturates so much of American life has shown that the passive approach to diversity, of just being different, is not and never will be enough. We need something more, and I have done my best to show why and also to show how. Ourselves among others—that's the wellspring of crafting a new diversity.

I would like to think that the well of American diversity is not poisoned, or if it is, that somehow we can pull off the impossible and *unpoison the well*. When I look out at the crowds that often come together to protest the things that seem broken in American society, the questions that are asked and the slogans that are shouted, on and on in an endless string of locutions, it is as if race, or something like race, is the only idiom we have to talk about ourselves among others. If it isn't race, it is some other simplified version of what we are. Diversity right now is such a limited idiom, a poor and ineloquent language that can never come close to describing all that we are and all that we can be. We need a new language to tell the tale of ourselves among others, and we all need to become *mutually* fluent in that language.

And we need to do this now because there is no better time than now, because there is no better place than here, because there is no better way than this, because the best we have done so far is not good enough, because the mistakes of the past cannot be allowed to undermine the present, because the mistakes of the present cannot be allowed to undermine the future, because mistrust is not a way of life, because racism is everywhere and should not be anywhere, because too many lives have been torn asunder and lost, because there is too much pride and not enough understanding, because we need to make a better world rather than just think it, because there is nothing to lose and everything to gain, because fear has kept us back for far too long, because hope has eluded us for even longer, because we've already waited long enough, because every excuse offered is an excuse that wastes our time, because talking the talk means nothing unless we walk the walk, because what is old can be made new, because what is broken can be fixed, because what is stale can be made fresh, because something better is worth fighting for, because reaching up is better than falling down, because reaching out is better than holding back, because the shoulder we lean on today leans back on us tomorrow, because three steps forward and two steps back is still one step forward no matter how small that is, because we have to expect from ourselves the things we expect from others, because we have to keep trying and trying and trying, because everyone is tired though there is so much left to do, because everything we do is at least something more, and because anything less is nothing at all.

INDEX

A
All Lives Matter
    as non-discrimination, 92
American Sauce
    as abomination, 72-73
anti-racial America
    vs. post-racial, 110
Asian Values
    and human rights, 23-25
Aung San Suu Kyi, 26

B
Bangkok Conference (1993), 21-23
Black Lives Matter
    as prioritization, 93
Boston Marathon bombing, 171
Bruce, Lenny, 59-60

C
Chappelle, Dave, 60-61
Chaudhry, Mahendra
    and Fiji coup, 14
chino
    as mistaken label, 20
Colombia
    and racism, 116-117
comedy
    and diversity, 57-59
Consistency Test, 138

D
Diversity Contribution Score
    at universities, 167
diversity hires
    new approach to, 152-153

E
enclaves
    identity-based, 46
    of laughter, 57
    political, 50
English
    as first language, 47
ethnic identity
    and establishing authenticity, 99
exclusion
    and identity, 101

F
Fujimori, Alberto, 15-18

G
General-Specific Test, 140
gentrification, 133-135
Gervais, Ricky, 45
going back
    as problem, 5
gypsy
    as ethnic slur, 31

H
Howard University
    and diversity, 136

I
identity box
    new approach to, 166

J
jihad
    and freedom, 175

K
Kureishi, Hanif, 177

L
language
    and diversity, 34-36
law
    and justice, 87

M
Malaysia, 27-31
Martin, Trayvon
    trial and diversity, 84-88
microaggressions, 52

N
native pronunciation, 34-37
NBA
    and diversity, 159-161
Nottebohm, Frederic
    and citizenship, 102-104
N-word
    and hate speech, 128

O
Ondaatje, Michael, 178
Orlando nightclub shooting, 139
Oscars
    and diversity, 157-158

P
Parti Keadilan Rakyat
    and Malaysian identity, 29
Past and Present Test, 143-145
political correctness, 42-45
posturing
    and identity, 116-118
Private-Public Test, 122
privilege laundering, 116-117
Pryor, Richard, 60

R
racism
    new definition of, 105
Reciprocity Test, 132
religion
    and diversity, 176
reparations
    and slavery, 146-148

S
safe space
    new definition of, 54
safe spaces, 51
Sasaki, Hank, 7-9
Singapore, 26
Sivashankarapillai, Thakazhi, 33

T
The Triple Package (2013), 110-112
Tizon, Alex, 181-182
Tsurunen, Marutei, 8-11

U
undocumented immigrant
    vs. illegal immigrant, 122-124

W
Water Fountain Test, 127-132
white privilege, 113-115

Y
Yale University, 145

ABOUT THE AUTHOR

D. C. Zook is a writer, musician, and filmmaker who also happens to be a professor at the University of California, Berkeley, in the departments of Global Studies and Political Science. He writes both fiction and nonfiction, and cultivates both sense and nonsense. He is currently at work on two books, one on new frontiers of human rights and the other on the changing landscape of cybersecurity. He is also plotting his next novel, and plotting many other things as well.

Visit D. C. Zook at dczook.com

www.ingramcontent.com/pod-product-compliance
Lightning Source LLC
Chambersburg PA
CBHW051546020426
42333CB00016B/2123